THE
DUELLING
HANDBOOK

1829

THE

ONLY APPROVED GUIDE

THROUGH ALL THE

STAGES OF A QUARREL:

CONTAINING THE

ROYAL CODE OF HONOR;

REFLECTIONS UPON DUELLING;

AND THE

OUTLINE OF A COURT FOR THE
ADJUSTMENT OF DISPUTES;

WITH

ANECDOTES, DOCUMENTS AND CASES, INTEREST-
ING TO CHRISTIAN MORALISTS WHO DECLINE THE
COMBAT; TO EXPERIENCED DUELLISTS,
AND TO BENEVOLENT LEGISLATORS.

BY JOSEPH HAMILTON.

Author of "The School for Patriots,"
and other popular works.

"'Tis time we should decree what course to take."
"The Bane and Antidote are both before me"

London;

HATCHARD & SONS; BENTHAM & CO.
LIVERPOOL; AND MILLIKIN, DUBLIN.

1829.

THE
DUELLING
HANDBOOK

1829

JOSEPH HAMILTON

DOVER PUBLICATIONS, INC.
Mineola, New York

Bibliographical Note

This Dover edition, first published in 2007, is an unabridged republication of the work originally published as *The Only Approved Guide through All the Stages of a Quarrel: Containing the Royal Code of Honor; Reflections upon Duelling; and the Outline of a Court for the Adjustment of Disputes; With Anecdotes, Documents and Cases, Interesting to Christian Moralists Who Decline the Combat; to Experienced Duellists, and to Benevolent Legislators* by Hatchard & Sons, London; Bentham & Co., Liverpool; and Millikin, Dublin, in 1829.

Library of Congress Cataloging-in-Publication Data

Hamilton, Joseph
    [Only approved guide through all the stages of a quarrel]
    The duelling handbook, 1829 / Joseph Hamilton.
      p. cm.
    Originally published: The only approved guide through all the stages of a quarrel. London : Hatchard & Sons, 1829.
    ISBN 0-486-45468-1 (pbk.)
    1. Dueling. I. Title.
CR4579.H3 2007
394'.8—dc22

                                   2006047099

Manufactured in the United States of America
Dover Publications, Inc., 31 East 2nd Street, Mineola, N.Y. 11501

THIS VOLUME

IS MOST RESPECTFULLY INSCRIBED

TO THE

SOVEREIGNS, PRINCES, NOBLEMEN,

AND GENTLEMEN,

THROUGHOUT THE EARTH;

BUT

MORE ESPECIALLY TO THOSE WHO
HAVE CONSIDERED THE AUTHOR'S
HUMBLE LABOURS

AS DESERVING OF THEIR BEST

THANKS, HIGH APPROVAL,

AND

POLITE CO-OPERATION.

JOSEPH HAMILTON.

Annadale Cottage,
near Dublin.

Contents

Contents

THE POINT OF HONOUR

"'Tis time we should decree what course to take,
The foe advances on us." Addison.

THE princes, noblemen, and gentlemen of Christendom must
have ascertained, by reading or their own experience, that,
constituted as society at present is, they possess no adequate
security against a challenge or offence.

Major DAWSON, with whose courage and good humour we are
familiar, was challenged by a brother officer of equal rank, for
merely pressing him to take another goblet; and General BARRY
was challenged by a Captain SMITH, for refusing to take wine
with him at dinner in a steam-packet. The General in vain
attempted to excuse himself, by declaring that wine invariably
made him sick at sea. Dr. DODD says, "I have known a challenge
sent to a person for going out of the room abruptly, and leaving
a man of honour in the midst of a dissertation." We could name
a thousand instances like those,* which remind us of the quarrel between VIOLA and Sir ANDREW AGUE-CHEEK, in which the
latter says, "You broke my head for nothing;" and Viola replies,
"You drew your sword upon me without cause."

In the cabinet, the senate, and the courts; the masquerade,
the ball-room, and the theatre; the club-room, the tavern, and
the street; in every situation, and in every company, the inconsiderate behaviour of one individual may involve the feelings
and the existence of another.

---

*Colonel MONTGOMERY was killed in a duel about a dog; Capt. RAMSAY in one
about a servant; Sterne's father was wounded by a Capt. PHILLIPS, in a duel
about a goose; and there is a popular story of a gentleman who shot his adversary in consequence of mistaking anchovies for capers.

Members of the royal family, ministers of state, legislators, judges, and other public functionaries, who might well have pleaded their official situations, have yielded to the pressure of a practice which they secretly condemned. Even preachers of the gospel have engaged in single combat;* and General HAMILTON, after writing against duelling, was unfortunately tempted to meet AARON BURR, by whose hand he fell a victim, on the very spot where his son had fallen before him. Who, then, can justly be surprised if the youth of Oxford, Cambridge, Eton, Westminster, and minor schools, should frequently commit themselves in mortal combat? or that persons in more humble walks of life should hold themselves amenable to what the world has called the laws of honour, and

> "Stand at another bar than that of law?"

Born and educated in a country which has been emphatically called *The Land of Duel,* and acquainted with several of its most chivalrous inhabitants, a case of *point blank* pistols was almost our earliest boast. We have sometimes felt ourselves obliged to ask the reparation of an injury, or satisfaction for an offence; but with deep, deep, gratitude we here record the fact, that the controller of all human actions never saw those pistols levelled at a fellow-subject, a hostile message forwarded to our address, or a single shot discharged, when the counsel which we offered was adopted.†

---

*Captain CALLANAN asserted, that the Rev. Mr. SAURIN offered to throw by his cassock. The Rev. Mr. HODSON fought and wounded Mr. GRADY, at Boulogne, in August, 1827; and in October, 1825, the Rev. H. T. fought Colonel W., between St. Omers and Cassel, where both were wounded. In 1769, the Rev. Mr. GREEN fought Captain DOUGLAS, in Hyde Park; the Rev. Mr. BATE fought Mr. R., of the Morning Post, in the same park, upon the 14th of September, 1780. And in 1828, the Rev. Mr. CRESPIGNY was only restrained from fighting Mr. W. LONG WELLESLEY by the great discretion of the seconds.

†We have never written nor spoken an offensive word against a nation, an individual, or a body, which we would not now be happy to recall. The man who cannot emulate Moore's noble apology to the Duke of Richmond is deserving of compassion. "I shall at least," says the patriotic Melodist, "be forgiven by those who have ever impatiently longed for an opportunity of acknowledging a fault and repairing an injustice."

During the last thirty years, we have had much experience in the direction both of principals and seconds, and have held directly opposing sentiments upon the subject. For half that period, we have firmly believed, with others, that duelling was a kind of necessary evil, and the best corrector of some ills with which society abounded. Thank Heaven, we now hold very different doctrine on the subject; and, shocked by the atrocities of a thousand anecdotes and cases, which we have collected with a view to publication, we are desirous of slaying a desolating monster, or, at least, depriving it of its talons and its fangs. If we cannot persuade a fellow-citizen to abstain from the field, our solicitude would follow him as long as counsel might be useful in averting evils which are so frequently attendant on the *dernier resort*. We would impress upon the minds of sovereigns and of legislators, that individual feeling and domestic happiness do not enjoy the security of all those shields to which they justly are entitled. We would enrol the names of princes and of nobles, of private and of professional gentlemen, who are disposed to co-operate in the establishment of courts of honour, for the arbitration of disputes which may be capable of adjustment; and we would promote another institution, for the total abolition of a practice which, after much experience, conversation, and reflection, we conscientiously believe to be "more honoured in the breach than in the observance." Thus we would become all to all, that all might be preserved from insult, injury, and the melancholy consequences which are so frequently attendant upon single combat.

Before we composed our short reflections upon duelling, with a view to the total abolition of the practice, we carefully perused almost every publication which had appeared upon the subject, and endeavoured to condense into the smallest possible compass, all the arguments which had been urged by the Christian, the moralist, and the man of common sense. We sent copies of that work to several courts in Christendom, and were unsuccessful in our effort to induce a simultaneous movement on the subject. We found it was too generally considered, that "a practice sanctioned by time and precedent, which has withstood the raillery of the satirist, the terror of the penal laws, and the admonition of the pulpit, nay, the fear of a future state, could never be abolished." We found persons high in power thought, with JONAS HANWAY, that "while so many adopt false principles of action, it is impossible to eradicate this most pernicious custom." We found many were of opinion with Sir WALTER SCOTT, who, in his letter to us on the subject, says, "Doing the fullest justice to the philanthropy of your motives, I am still afraid that the practice of duelling is so deeply engrafted on the forms of society, that, for a length of time at least, until mankind may entertain much clearer views upon most moral subjects, it will hardly fall into disuse."

We know that two sovereigns of Christendom have committed themselves as principals, and that others have recognised the sad necessity of duelling. The editor of the Literary Gazette asserts, that on examining the correspondence of Lords WELLINGTON and WINCHILSEA, his Majesty expressed himself to the effect, that "it was a matter of personal honour and feeling, and that, being a soldier, his Grace might, perhaps, be more sensitive on such points that an individual of a different class in society. He therefore supposed, that the course pursued had been unavoidable."*

A London editor has very justly said, "Duels have become so common, that we cease almost to hear of their immediate causes. It is now deemed, by those who record passing occurrences, quite sufficient to say, that a meeting took place between two gentlemen, as if it were an interview of pleasant courtesy, instead of an arena, where either may too often exclaim, with Richard,

"Of one or both of us, the time is come."

When GEORGE ROBERT FITZGERALD was introduced to the King of France by the British Ambassador, his Majesty was

---

*Having been honoured by a kind assurance from the Duke of WELLINGTON, that he perused the Code of Honour with *great interest* at the period of its publication, we hoped that the hero of so many battles would have been governed by Article VIII, which recommends to public functionaries the sacrifice of private feeling to a sense of public duty.

M. CARON DE FROMENTELLE, the Procureur de Roi, when writing to the Rev. J. R. HODSON, a Protestant clergyman, who fought and wounded Mr. THOS. WM. GRADY, at Boulogne, says, the parson "yielded to a barbarous prejudice, unfortunately not to be gotten rid of."

informed that the Irishman had fought six-and-twenty fatal duels. Lieut. C——KS, of the navy, fought three duels in a day. BARRINGTON says, two hundred and twenty-seven memorable and official duels were fought during his grand climacteric. A single writer enumerates one hundred and seventy-two duels, in which sixty-three individuals were killed, and ninety-six wounded; in three of those cases both the combatants were slain, and eighteen of the survivors received the sentence of the laws they had transgressed. We can produce four newspapers which announce twelve fatal meetings on the ground.* Surely then, we may assert, with SHAKESPEARE'S JULIUS CÆSAR, that

"Slaying is the word; it is a deed of fashion."

Having failed in our endeavours to promote the abolition of the practice, we were next induced to try if we could lessen its attendant evils. We found, in several thousand anecdotes and cases, which we had collected during thirty years, a mass of evidence that the grossest atrocities and errors were committed hourly on the subject. We conceived that such atrocities and errors might possibly in future be prevented, by the extensive circulation of a well-digested code of laws, in which the highest tone of chivalry and honour might be intimately associated with justice, humanity and common sense; and we were encouraged by several experienced friends, as well as by Plato's strong assurance, that it is truly honourable to contrive how the worst things can be turned into better.

After carefully perusing our collection of remarkable quarrels, challenges, replies, rencontres, duels, and reconciliations, we sketched out a code, consisting of twenty articles, which we submitted to experienced friends in Ireland. We next forwarded manuscript copies to the first political, military, and literary characters of the age, and received the most complimentary assurances of approbation. In May, 1824, we forwarded printed copies for the several courts of Europe and America, as well as

---

*The Dublin Correspondent of 20th September, and the Dublin Morning Post of the 25th September, 1823, the Dublin Freeman's Journal of August 12th, 1824, and the London Sun of April 3rd, are the papers alluded to.

to the conductors of the public press, for the purpose of inducing the transmission of such corrections and additions as might, if possible, render it deserving of universal acceptation; and we have now the satisfaction of presenting to the world a collection of highly-applauded rules, for the government of principals and seconds, in our ROYAL CODE OF HONOUR.

We should weary the reader, were we to publish all the complimentary letters which we have received, from princes, noblemen, statesmen, officers, and others, for our public labours upon this important subject;* a few of them, however, may suffice to recommend our works, and to justify us for submitting to the world, the only approved guide through all the stages of a quarrel, for the advocate of single combat, and for the Christian moralist who scruples fighting.

The following has been copied from the letter of Colonel SHAW, secretary to the Marquis WELLESLEY, when that accomplished nobleman was viceroy of Ireland.

"Woodstock, Nov. 15, 1823.

"I have had the honour to lay before the Lord Lieutenant your letter of the 12th instant, together with your work on Duelling, for which I am desired to return you to his Excellency's best thanks, and to express you his approbation of the laudable object of that publication. I have the honour to be, Sir, your most obedient, humble servant,

"M. SHAWE."

JOSEPH HAMILTON, ESQ.
Annadale Cottage, near Dublin.

---

*Our truly estimable and respected friend, the Rev. Dr. BURTON, assistant chaplain to the Dublin garrison, has been pleased to call our reflections upon duelling, "The Annual Hamiltonian Præmium;" and we value the compliment more highly on account of his general devotion to the advancement of his pupils, whom he treats invariably as if they were his children.

We could quote innumerable instances of fatal duels between fellow-students at colleges, and very young classmates at schools, which would justify us in recommending parents and teachers to adopt our publication as a præmium book, or keepsake, for the youth beneath their care.

Two boys, aged 16, named WETHERALL and MORAN, fought near Mark's Church, Dublin. Two boys of the same age, who had been expelled from

A nobleman, and general officer, who has fired eight shots in a single duel, says,

> "I have been favoured with yours of the 26th ultimo, together with the accompanying inclosures; in reply, I beg leave to say, that the proposed association shall have my support, and I shall be much obliged to you to send me a dozen copies of the work."

Another nobleman, who is equally respected for his patriotism and exalted sense of honour, says,

> "I admire extremely and approve of your benevolent exertions to put an end to the barbarous system of duelling; but I fear that, barbarous though it be, it is the means of civilization, and acts as a kind of safety-valve to the ebullition of passion. Many despotic, and many wise and liberal princes, have endeavoured to put an end to the practice, but in vain; and when they have failed, I fear that any exertions of mine, even with your assistance, would prove altogether ineffectual. If, however, two men of known and respected character, and two military men, join in such endeavour, I shall not object to lend my feeble assistance."

Extract from the letter of the Rev. CHARLES BARDIN:

"Dear Sir,
    "I have received your very beautiful little book. May your purpose meet with that blessing which its benevolence deserves. I have the honor to be, dear Sir, your faithful servant,
                                        "CHARLES BARDIN."

Yale College, fought with rifles, at the distance of twenty paces; they were encouraged by their parents, one of whom was witness to the death of his son. Two pupils of the Polytecnic School, aged 17, fought in the Bois de Boulogne, when one of the seconds was mortally wounded, by standing too near his principal. If duels between persons of very tender age are calculated to excite our sorrow, what feelings of indignation must be roused on the perusal of some cases, in which near relations—kinsmen, and brothers, have been allowed to slay each other?

The ROYAL CODE OF HONOUR having been submitted, both in manuscript and print, to the late Duke of York, as chief commander of the army, he was pleased to direct the following reply from the Horse Guards.

"Sir,—I am directed by the Commander-in-chief to acknowledge the receipt of your letter of the 8th ultimo, and to return you his Royal Highness's thanks for your attention, in sending him a copy of your valuable publication, entitled the Royal Code of Honour, &c. I have the honour to be, Sir, your most obedient, humble servant,

"H. TAYLOR."

Extract of a letter from Sir WALTER SCOTT, Bart.:

"The advice to seconds appears most excellent, and the Code of Honour seems highly capable of softening the atrocities of our gothic custom."

Extract of a letter from Captain FOTTRELL, of Dublin:

"Dear Sir,

I have received with gratitude your two publications, the *School for Patriots,* and *Royal Code of Honour.* With attention I have perused the latter, which consists of *sixty articles, to every one of which* I most *heartily* subscribe.

"There are few men in Dublin, or perhaps in Ireland, who have been more engaged in the adjustment of misunderstandings, than I have; and by the adoption of similar principles to those which you have laid down, I have the happiness (thank God,) to say, that in almost every case, amicable arrangements have taken place, and *in no instance* has recourse been had to those evils which it is your object to avoid.

"The *Christian* and *philanthropic* principles which prompted you to bring before the public this little *(though great)* work, entitles you to their gratitude. Believe me very sincerely yours,

"PATRICK FOTTRELL."

In Dublin it would be needless to assert, that the writer of the last letter is one of the most honourable individuals who has ever been placed in the situation of a principal or second. His desperate duel with Colonel Ross, when he stood as a champion for the press, will be found in our collection.

Other testimonials, with the names of such sovereigns, princes, noblemen, and gentlemen, as approve of courts of honor, or anti-duelling associations, will be published at the conclusion of the work, with a copious Index to the numerous anecdotes, cases, and authorities which it will contain, for the fire-eater, the peace-maker, the legislator, and the lawyer.

The work is already in a very forward state, and may be inspected by any person who is interested on the subject. It will consist of four very neat duodecimo volumes, price one pound. The profits will be usefully applied. All communications and orders for this work, the School for Patriots, and the authors' other publications,* may be addressed, in free letters, for JOSEPH HAMILTON, Annadale Cottage, near Dublin.

---

*On Prevailing Vices; the Presence of God; Innocent Convicts; Capital Punishment; War; Slavery; Christian Union; the Temporal and Spiritual Restoration of Israel; Irish History; Hebrew History; Lost Ark Tribes, &c.; Friendship, Love and Marriage; Scraps found in the Portfolio of Captain Rock; Useful Gleanings; Letters, Poems, &c.

THE
DUELLING
HANDBOOK
1829

THE ROYAL CODE OF HONOR

"Honor's not captious, nor dispos'd to fight,
But, seeks to shun what's wrong, and do what's right."

I.

No duel can be considered justifiable, which can be declined with honor, therefore, an appeal to arms should always be the last resource.*

II.

When a gentleman receives a blow, or any other provocation, he should immediately retire, without making the slightest retort; a line of conduct which is truly noble; which can never increase the breach, nor embarrass the question as to the first aggression; and which must always prepare the offender's mind for his offering reparation, either before, or after he may be required to do so.

III.

In a case which appears to require recurrence to a duel, the challenge should always emanate from the individual who first conceives himself offended.

---

*Should any individual attempt to deviate from rules which have been so very highly sanctioned by the chief commander of the British army, and others whose letters we have inserted in the introduction, his adversary will be justified in refusing to recognize him as a gentleman; and should any case arise which has not been provided for sufficiently, it should be referred to arbitrators, or to a court of honor, which we can convene in London or in Dublin.

1

IV.

Honor and revenge have no alliance; therefore, reparation for offence or injury, is all that can be fairly sought for, or conceded.

V.

The "gate of mercy" should never be closed, nor an aggressor's passage over the "golden bridge" obstructed; on the contrary, he should in every stage of the negociation, or duel, be won to a consideration of his duty, by the utmost delicacy and politeness.

VI.

Every apology which may be proposed, should be as dignified as the nature of the circumstances will admit of, it being inconsistent with true honor, to attempt the unnecessary degradation of an adversary.

VII.

An injury sustained by an individual in his property, can never be a proper subject for a duel.

VIII.

When a gentleman is the depository of any public trust, it is more honorable to sacrifice his individual feelings, than the general interests of society.*

---

*Having been honored by a kind assurance from the Duke of WELLINGTON, that he perused the Code of Honor with *great interest* at the period of its publication, we hoped that the hero of so many battles would have been governed by Article VIII. which recommends for public functionaries the sacrifice of private feeling to a sense of public duty.

The correspondence, however, with Lord Winchilsea, justifies the assertion of his Grace, that he neglected nothing to effect an amicable adjustment of the business. A court of honor would soon have disembarrassed both the parties.

IX.

Professional gentlemen, on whose energies or talents, the lives, fortunes, or reputation of their clients may depend, can never justify their fighting duels, without making a full, and timely surrender of their trusts.

X.

Public functionaries, such as Cabinet Ministers, Judges, Senators, Officers, Magistrates, Jurors, and Proprietors, or Editors of Literary Works, are justified in preserving their perfect independence, by the refusal of all challenges, founded on the mere discharge of public duty. A Barrister may justify interrogatories, or assertions, which affect the character, or feelings of a Witness or Suitor, by the production of a pleading, or a brief; and a Solicitor may transfer responsibility from himself, by exhibiting the written instructions from his Client, to put such interrogatories, or to make such assertions. This article cannot however, be taken as justifying either abuse, or personality, which every well-bred gentleman, will be studious to avoid.*

XI.

If Marcus receive an offence from Julius, and would remove the stain which he conceives attaches to his honor, his success in doing so, will invariably bear an exact proportion to the gentlemanly delicacy of his own behaviour.

XII.

If Marcus, in order to throw upon the first aggressor, the supposed necessity for originating the challenge, shall proceed to horse whip Julius, strike him with his fist, a stick, or even

---

*In the first edition of this Code, the following sentence formed Article II. "Every gentleman should carefully abstain from nicknames, mimickry, offensive jokes, and what is usually termed horse-play, as in the imprudent indulgence of such very vulgar follies, irreconcilable quarrels but too frequently originate." It has however been advisedly displaced, to make room for the more important one which now forms Article X.

his glove; call him liar, coward, or by any other irritating appellation, he does not efface the stain, which he imagines his reputation has contracted; but on the contrary he considerably aggravates it, by descending to a violence of action, or expression, which every well bred gentleman is habitually anxious to avoid, and by associating with his conduct the recollection, that violence is almost invariably resorted to by persons whose bodily strength, or pugilistic science, gives them a considerable advantage over the gentlemen they are determined to assail.*

XIII.

When any gentleman neglects the honorable line of conduct, which is suggested in the 2nd and 11th Articles, and adopts that which is the subject of the 12th, he ought not to feel himself aggrieved, if he be brought before a very different tribunal, from that to which he certainly aspires unjustly.

XIV.

It is the duty of every gentleman, who experiences such violent, or abusive treatment, as has been noticed in Article 2nd, to let his assailant suffer under the influence of the stain, supposed to have been imparted by the original offence, and to seek redress for the assault, or the abusive language, from the Courts of Law, in order to suppress a violence, which is injurious to civilized society.

XV.

A gentleman who values his own reputation very highly, will not fight a duel with, nor act as Second to, a person who has been guilty of the conduct alluded to in Article the 12th, or of any other offence against the public morals.

---

* "One outrage (says Rousseau) committed in return for another, does not annul the first. He who receives the first insult, is the only person offended."

XVI.

The utmost caution should always be observed in the selection of a Second; if possible he should be, a "man who is not passion's slave, a man who may be worn in a heart's core, aye, in a heart of hearts."[*]

XVII.

No gentleman should accept the office of a Second, without first receiving from his friend, a written statement of the case upon his honor, which should be accessible to both the Seconds, for facilitating an accommodation, and justifying the conduct of the Principals, as well as that of the Seconds, in the event of a fatal termination to the quarrel. Every Second should also insist upon receiving a written consent, to offer, or receive such apology, submission, or explanation, as may be confidentially agreed upon, between the Principal and himself, there being melancholy instances upon record, in which the Principals have converted Seconds into mere automatons at their own command.

XVIII.

The Principals and their Seconds should always hold in their remembrance, that the most trifling expression, look, or gesture,

---

[*]It is with considerable pain, but with a sense of public duty, that in this edition we censure the behaviour of Mr. Bric's second, upon an occasion which proved fatal to the learned gentleman. There scarcely ever was a case which afforded more facilities for an adjustment. Mr. Bric was an admirer of this Code, he and his antagonist were reasonable men, their quarrel was accidental, about a third person, and happened in the warmth of electioneering zeal. A very trifling explanation would have saved the life of Bric, and the reputation of his second. Had we been upon the ground, we would have stood between the combatants, and prevented the effusion of that blood which we afterwards saw congealed. Doubtless Mr. Gregg, the second to Mr. Hayes, has frequently regretted that his not meeting Mr. Fitzgerald, and an observance of too much etiquette, should have increased the difficulties of this very simple case. We shall shew a grievous error on the part of Mr. Bric's adviser in the field, to which the learned gentleman was probably indebted for his death.

may be subject to the strictest scrutiny, before a Court and Jury, as well as before the world, and their ***

XIX.

The Principals and their Seconds, should be careful to make notes of every circumstance connected with the management of the quarrel, duel, or negociation, with particular attention to time, place, language, gesture, tone and witnesses.

XX.

If the receiver of a challenge, shall refuse to give a meeting on account of any alleged unworthiness in the rank or character of the challenger, he cannot be justified in offering an insinuation that he is willing to meet the Second, or another gentleman, on behalf of him who has been slighted; for by doing so, he very wantonly provokes an unoffending person, who may have a very high opinion of the character which is aspersed.

XXI.

When a gentleman shall be unjustly aspersed, under the circumstances described in the last Article, he may be effectually vindicated by the testimonials of his friends, and the aggressor may be left to the enjoyment of the public impression, respecting his courage, generosity, and justice.

XXII.

The bearer of a slighted message, cannot be justified in considering himself offended, if he be treated with politeness; because the character of his friend is a mere matter of opinion, upon which two very estimable gentlemen may differ, and it must always be a censurable intolerance, which would attempt to force upon one man's mind, even the correct opinion of another.

XXIII.

No gentleman, who values his own reputation very highly, will refuse to receive, or offer such reparation, as may be mutually agreed upon between the Seconds.

XXIV.

When bosom friends, fathers of large, or unprovided families, or very inexperienced youths are about to fight, the Seconds must be doubly justified in their solicitude for reconciliation.*

XXV.

When giving the lie, or using any other irritating language, has been the first aggression, if it appear, that such language was resorted to under any erroneous impression, and that such impression has been satisfactorily removed by explanation, the written expression of sincere regret, for the use of such provoking language, may be offered, and accepted, consistently with the most honorable feelings; but can never with propriety be either refused, or delayed.

XXVI.

An apology, with its usual accompaniment, the offer of a whip or switch, should always be accepted for a blow, or for any other offence, which may be considered an assault.

XXVII.

The handing of a horsewhip, or a stick to a person who has been assaulted, may be dispensed with, at the solicitation of the offending party, and upon the written plea of his hazarding his commission, rank, pay, or family expectance.†

---

*We can furnish several cases, in which a message has been withdrawn, in order to promote a reconciliation; this, however, must be done with an understanding that the challenger does not forego his claim.

†We shall justify this by cases which are before us.

XXVIII.

If any gentleman shall be so unfortunate as to assault another, it is much more honorable for him to offer the usual accompaniment, a whip or a stick with his apology, than to neglect a reparation which the public opinion so very firmly demands.

XXIX.

A Principal should not be allowed to wear light coloured clothing, ruffles, military decorations, or any other very attractive object, upon which the eye of his antagonist may rest.

XXX.

The squibbing or trying of pistols on the ground, or in its vicinity, should never be permitted, and there never should be two cases of pistols loaded at a time, as the delay in loading, between the discharge of shots, may afford facilities for reconciliation.

XXXI.

If a duel should originate in a wanton charge of cowardice, it is not necessary that the offended party should vindicate his courage by standing many shots; on the contrary, he may leave the ground with honor after the first discharge, even though his adversary, forgetful of his duty, should refuse to retract, and apologize for an accusation so ungenerously preferred.

XXXII.

If a gentleman be urged or allowed to fight, who is in liquor, unprepared with a confidential Second, or who has not had sufficient time to make a proper disposition of his property and trusts, for the advantage of his family, constituents, clients, wards, or creditors,° a suspicion of foul play must inevitably

---

°We are collecting the names of surgeons and attorneys who may be advantageously consulted on the point of honor, as well as upon their own professional business.

attach itself to all persons by whom it may be sanctioned, suggested, or even witnessed without opposition.

XXXIII.

If a challenged party shall refuse the satisfaction which may be required, a simple notification of the facts, through any public journal, will be far more creditable to the challenger, than personal violence, or what is usually termed posting.

XXXIV.

The Second of the party who has been challenged, should invariably have the appointment of the time and place of meeting. The scene of action should be as convenient as possible to both the combatants, especially to surgical assistance; and all extravagant propositions should be carefully rejected, such as fighting across a table, at handkerchief's length, or hand to hand; using daggers, knives, rifles, blunderbusses, &c.

XXXV.

As the death of an individual may sometimes bring party feelings into action, a meeting should be as private as possible, consistently with all the circumstances of the case.

XXXVI.

The boundary of the county in which the offence was given, should not be crossed, except in the avoidance of pursuit, or in cases where very strong popular feeling may exist in favour of a Principal.

XXXVII.

In choosing the scene of action, special precaution should invariably be used, to prevent the necessity for carrying wounded gentlemen over walls, ditches, gates, stiles, or hedges; or too great a distance to a dwelling.

XXXVIII.

The parties should invariably salute each other at their meeting on the ground, and they should be emulous in offering this evidence of civilization, remembering that they have, by the very act of meeting, made an acknowledgment of equality, and evinced a perfect willingness to receive, or offer, the supposed necessary reparation.

XXXIX.

Until a perfect reconciliation shall have been agreed upon, a Principal should avoid all conversation with his adversary;° the Seconds should invariably be the organs of their Principals, and every conversation between a Principal and his Second should be so perfectly apart, as to preclude the opposite party from recognizing their words, looks, or gestures.

XL.

Every choice, or advantage, which may present itself upon the ground, should be invariably decided by the toss of three, five, or seven coins, after they have been carefully shaken in a hat.

XLI.

The challenged party should have the first toss, the challenger the second, and so on in alternate succession, as long as any choice, or advantage, shall remain to be decided.

XLII.

No boast, threat, trick, or stratagem, which may wound the feelings, or lessen the equality of the combatants, should ever enter into the contemplation of a gentleman.

°The neglect of this rule exposed Mr. Battier to irreparable inconvenience.

XLIII.

No gentleman should be permitted to wear spectacles, or an eyeglass on the ground, but such as habitually use them in the public streets.

XLIV.

Gentlemen who do not set a very exorbitant value upon their time and labour, will avoid refusing, even upon the ground, such an apology, as they would have accepted in the earlier stages of negociation.*

XLV.

The parties should never be allowed to fight at less than ten yards distance, to be always well defined by toe-stones, for the advanced feet of the combatants; and as duelling pistols, will inflict a mortal wound at more than forty yards, very trivial differences may be terminated at that distance.

XLVI.

If unfortunately, swords should be preferred to pistols, the ground should be clean, dry, and even, and the combatants stationed so far asunder, that neither can possibly take the other by surprise.

XLVII.

If the parties are to fight with pistols, they should never be stationed in highways, footpaths, under walls or hedges, or along the ridges of a field, as all right lines contribute to the guidance of the weapon, and expose the parties to a danger, which is at least unnecessary.

---

*We shall furnish plenty of precedents for amicable settlements upon the ground.

XLVIII.

No duel should be fought on Sunday, or on a Festival; for twenty-four hours after the challenge is delivered; nor near a place of public worship; and before the parties are permitted to fire, they should be cautioned not to pass the toe-stones or stakes which mark the measured distance.

XLIX.

The Seconds should stand between the Principals thus:

P. S. . . . . .S. P.

when conferring with, or presenting pistols to them, and the feather springs should not be set.

L.

The signal should be a white handkerchief, or other very attractive object, placed upon the ground, exactly midway between the Principals, that each may have a view of it, and that one of the Seconds may withdraw it at his pleasure by a cord.

LI.

The Seconds should meet at the white handkerchief in the centre, thus:

P . . . . .S. h. S . . . . .P.

during every conference with each other on the ground, and while they are loading the pistols.

LII.

Previous to the moving of the handkerchief, the Seconds should retire from the centre, at right angles, to the sides on which they may be conveniently observed by the respective Principals, thus:—*

---

*We have several cases in which seconds have been killed or wounded.

S.
.
.
.
.
.
.
.
.
.
.
.
.

P . . . . h. . . . . .P.

.
.
.
.
.
.
.
.
.
.
.
.
S.

LIII.

Previous to the moving of the handkerchief, the Second of the challenger, should again solicit reparation for his friend, and if the parties still continue obstinate, he should enquire distinctly, if they are prepared.

LIV.

The parties should present and fire together, at the signal previously agreed on, without resting on their aim, or they should lose their right to fire; and firing by word of command, should be invariably avoided, as in such cases, unnecessary danger is incurred, by permitting the eye to make a preparatory rest upon its object.

LV.

The Seconds should mutually and zealously attempt a reconciliation after every discharge of pistols; but this is always the indispensable duty of the Second to him who has received the challenge.°

LVI.

Neither an Aggressor, nor his Second, can ever be justified for endangering the life of a gentleman, who may have been assaulted, injured, or offended.†

LVII.

Neither Principal, nor Second, can justify the abandonment of a gentleman who may be wounded, without previously securing for him a proper conveyance from the field; for the retreat of a brave man, should always be as dignified as his advance.

LVIII.

When the quarrel shall have terminated, the Seconds should remind the friends and relatives of the combatants, that the

---

°Surgeons who, like the late John Adrien and his son, are as well acquainted with the point of honor as with gunshot wounds, may offer their conciliatory suggestions when attending *reasonable gentlemen.* Mr. Hume went farther, he even charged the pistols for Lords Wellington and Winchilsea. Indeed all by standers, may in some degree be considered as the representatives of that public, in whose estimation every gentleman should be anxious to stand well; and being much less interested than the principals or seconds, their temperate interference may be justly influential in the happy termination of a quarrel.
†Gentlemen who make immediate reparation when applied to, must derive considerable satisfaction from the recollection of their having spared the friends and relatives of both the parties, that great anxiety which is usually excited by the knowledge of a quarrel and the prospect of a hostile meeting in the field. Such a line of conduct is far preferable to the standing for a shot, and the discharging of a pistol in the air. Surely if reparation should be made it cannot be made too soon.

slightest indiscretion in their conversation on the subject, may renew the breach, and render a second meeting fatal.

LIX.

When a reconciliation* shall have been effected, or a duel terminated, the Principals should very carefully abstain from conversation upon the subject, always referring, if it should be necessary, to the Seconds, or to their written testimonials.

LX.

Finally, as the reputation of each party, at the termination of a quarrel, or a duel, must bear an exact proportion to the respectable behaviour of the other; neither a Principal nor his Second, can boast of any triumph or advantage, without a considerable abatement of his glory, as well as an abandonment of that chivalrous generosity, which must for ever be inseparable from the Point of Honor. The Author of DOUGLAS declares, that

"The noblest vengeance is the most complete."

And another judicious writer has observed, that

"Cowards are cruel; but the brave
Love mercy, and delight to save."

Let every gentleman, then, who may be jealous of his honor, be careful not to tarnish it, by the means which he adopts for its support: let him say with Sheridan, "To judge the action, I must know the means;" or with Addison,

---

*Nothing is more moving to a man than the spectacle of reconciliation: our weaknesses are indemnified, and are not too costly—being the price we pay for the hour of forgiveness: and the archangel who has never felt anger, has reason to envy the man who subdues it. When thou forgivest—the man, who has pierced thy heart, stands to thee in the relation of a sea-worm that perforates the shell of the muscle, which straightway closes the wound with a pearl.

"Honor's a sacred tie, the law of Kings,
The noble mind's distinguishing perfection,
That aids and strengthens virtue, where it meets her,
And imitates her actions, where she is not;
It ought not to be sported with."

JOSEPH HAMILTON

Annadale Cottage,
near Dublin.

SOME SHORT AND USEFUL
REFLECTIONS UPON DUELLING

*"Learn, mortals, from my precepts to control
The furious passions, which disturb the soul."*

As I know not the moment I may receive a challenge, or an offence—and as a timely preparation of my mind, must give me a fair advantage over my antagonist, I will now give the subject of Duelling a dispassionate consideration, and carefully treasure for an angry moment, the useful reflections of a tranquil one.

The advocates for the custom allege in its defence, that it places all gentlemen upon an equal footing; and that according to the prevailing notions of worldly honor, a challenge cannot be refused, nor an insult overlooked.°

°A friend and relative of Mr. Hanway's was challenged by a man whom he had never seen nor heard of. As a man of the sword, however, he consented, and had the fortune to make his antagonist beg his life; this person then confessed, that he had no other motive for fighting but his distressed condition, and intreated his antagonist to assist him. The wounds he had received now made him a greater object of compassion; so that this extravagant enterprise ended in the aggressor's being relieved by the charity of the man whom he had provoked to this desperate trial of his skill.

Dr. Dodd gives the following answer to a challenge:—"Sir,—Your behaviour last night has convinced me that you are a scoundrel; and your letter this morning that you are a fool. If I should accept your challenge, I should myself be both. I owe a duty to God and my country, which I deem it infamous to violate; and I am intrusted with a life, which I think cannot, without folly, be staked against your's. I believe you have ruined, but you cannot degrade me. You may possibly, while you sneer over this letter, secretly exult in your own

Not one of those, I believe, has ventured to assert, that it is consistent with either law, morality, or religion; but that it is contrary to all those three, as well as to common sense and real honor, has been alleged by numbers.

That duelling is contrary to common sense has been insisted on for the following reasons:

---

savage heart; but remember, that to prevent assassination, I have a sword; and to chastise insolence, a cane.

Gaston, Marquis de Renty, an illustrious nobleman, was a soldier and a Christian; and possessed a very happy disposition to reconcile the seeming opposition between those two characters. He had a command in the French army, and was so unfortunate as to receive a challenge from a person of distinction in the same service. The Marquis replied, he was ready to convince the challenger that he was in the wrong; or, if he could not convince him, he was as ready to ask his pardon. The other, not being satisfied with this, insisted upon his meeting him with the sword; to which the Marquis sent him the following message: that "he was resolved not to comply with the demand, since God and his sovereign had forbidden it; otherwise he would speedily convince him that all the efforts he had used to pacify him did not proceed from the fear of fighting. That he should go every day about his usual business, and would be prepared to defend himself against any assault which he might experience." The parties met soon after, and the Marquis being compelled to draw in his defence, with the assistance of a servant, soon wounded and disarmed both the assailant and his second. The Marquis then conducted his opponents to his own tent, where, after refreshing them with cordials and seeing that their wounds were dressed, he restored the swords which they had forfeited in the combat, dismissed them with advice which became a Christian and a gentleman, and could never afterwards be prevailed upon to mention the trifling circumstance connected with his triumph. This brave nobleman used frequently to observe, "That there was more true courage and generosity in bearing and forgiving an injury, for the love of God, than in requiting it with another; in suffering, rather than in revenging; because the thing was really more difficult." Adding, "That bulls and bears had courage enough, but it was a brutal courage; whereas that of men should be such as became rational beings.

A certain manuscript of Jonas Hanway's, clandestinely taken and misrepresented, gave an alarm to a gentleman of the fighting sort, upon which Mr. Hanway received a letter conceived in these terms.

Sir,—I understand you are the author of a paper subscribed ° ° ° ° in which are initial letters that I presume mean me. As I always make it a point to resent affronts, I desire you will meet me at ° ° ° ° and bring your sword with you.

I am, &c.

First, It cannot place the combatants upon an equal footing, for all men have not equal nerves, sight, or size, and some can slit a dozen bullets on a sabre's edge, or send them through a key-hole, while others could not wound an elephant in an hundred efforts.

Second, It is as imprudent to give a man, who has already

To which the following answer was returned.

Sir,—In reply to your letter, the meaning of which I suppose is a challenge to fight with you; as I do not know by what authority you call me to account, I will not tell you whether I am the author of any such paper as you mention, or not; but this I think my honour is concerned to tell you, that I never intend to do any man an injury; and if an offence does come, that honour also obliges me to make attonement, without putting my friends to the trouble of fighting; and for my part, I always make it a point not to resent affronts, beyond the measure which reason and religion warrant.

As to meeting you at ° ° ° ° I have no inclination to walk in such bad weather as this, much less am I disposed to fight for nothing; but a sword I always wear, intending to use it upon every just occasion.   I am, & c.

In this case, says Mr. Hanway, my antagonist was satisfied, and no doubt was glad to be excused from fighting, as all men are except those who are intoxicated with wine, or what is much the same, with anger, or quite deprived of understanding. I will suppose I had the same sort of sense as my adversary, and had carried my sword as he desired, used it and died, and been brought to my last account, for such account I believe there will be, what could I say in my own defence? that I was not afraid of God; but I feared the phantom of opinion. But what if I had killed my adversary, and to put the matter in the best light, been pardoned by human laws, could all my tears of repentance have cleansed my hand from this honorable murder. Ought I not to run it into the flames, and stand as a Roman did upon a worse occasion, to see it burnt off to expiate the bloody deed, if such an expiation could avail.

Sir Richard Steele appears by his own words to have fought off several fool-hardy geniuses who were for "trying their valour on him," supposing a saint was necessarily a poltroon. Thus the Christian hero finding himself slighted by his loose companions, sat down and composed a most laughable comedy.

A celebrated literary gentleman had a quarrel with one of his acquaintances; the latter concluded a note upon the subject with the following expression,—"I have a life at your service, if you dare take it." To which the other replied, "You say you have a life at my service if I dare take it. I must confess to you that I dare not take it. I thank my God, that I have not the courage to take it. But though I own that I am afraid to deprive you of your

wronged me, an opportunity of doing me a further injury, as it would to trust with one thousand pounds a person who had already ran away with ten.

Third, If my adversary be a worthless man, I shall degrade my own character effectually by placing it upon a level with his; and if, on the contrary, he be an estimable character, I should not

---

life, yet, permit me Sir to assure you, that I am equally thankful to the Almighty Being, for mercifully bestowing on me sufficient resolution if attacked to defend my own." This spirited reply produced the desired effect; reason resumed her seat, friends interfered, and the difference was adjusted.

An American gentleman sent the following good-humoured answer to a challenge:—"I have two objections to this duel matter: the one is lest I should hurt you, and the other is lest you should hurt me. I do not see any good it would do me to put a bullet through any part of your body: I could make no use of you when dead for any culinary purpose, as I could of a rabbit or a turkey. I am no cannibal to feed upon the flesh of men! Why then should I shoot down a human creature, of which I could make no use? A buffalo would be better meat, for though your flesh might be delicate and tender, yet it wants that firmness and consistency which takes and retains salt. At any rate it would not be fit for long voyages. You might make a good barbicue, it is true, being of the nature of a racoon or an opossum; but people are not in the habit of barbicuing any thing human now. As to your hide it is not worth taking off, being little better than that of a year old colt. As to myself, I do not wish to stand in the way of any thing harmful; I am under an apprehension you might hit me; that being the case, I think it most advisable to stay at a distance. If you want to try your pistol, take some object, a tree, or a barn door, about my dimensions. If you hit that send me word, and I shall acknowledge, that if I had been in the same place you might have hit me."

When Augustus Cæsar received a challenge from Anthony to fight a duel, he very calmly replied, "If Anthony is weary of his life, tell him there are other ways to death than the point of my sword."

The brave Sir Sidney Smith, during the siege of Acre, sent a message to Napoleon, who replied, that if the gallant knight wished to amuse himself, he would chalk out a few yards of neutral ground, and send him a grenadier, whose size should increase the chances of being hit; adding, that if Sir Sidney shot his representative, he would candidly allow him all the advantages of the victory; but that he had at that time too much business upon his hands, in directing the physical energies of his country, to indulge in the amusements of a school-boy. Such was the general report of this transaction at the time of its occurrence; but in the Anecdotes we have given Napoleon's own description of it.

Jonas Hanway says, a friend of his knew a case in which the challenged

stand upon a nice punctilio with him, while he is under the influence of a momentary fever.

Duels for private quarrels were so repugnant to common sense, that they were not practised by the Greeks, Romans, or

---

party cried out in a public coffee house, "You ° ° ° °, what do you mean by sending me a challenge; do you think that at my time of life, I am such a fool as to fight a duel."

At a meeting under a commission of bankrupt, in Andover, between Mr. Fleet and Mr. Mann, both respectable solicitors of that town, some disagreement arose, which ended in the former sending the latter a challenge, to which the following poetic answer was returned:—

TO KINGSTON FLEET, ESQ.

I am honor'd this day, sir, with challenges two,
The first from friend Langdon, the second from you;
As the one is to *fight,* and the other to *dine,*
I accept *his* "engagement," and your's must decline.

Now, in giving this preference, I trust you'll admit
I have acted with prudence, and done what was fit;
Since encountering *him,* and my weapon a knife,
There is some little chance of *preserving* my life,
Whilst a bullet from you, Sir, *might* take it away,
And the maxim, you know, is to live while we may.

If, however, you still should suppose I ill treat you,
By sternly rejecting this challenge to meet you,
Bear with me a moment, and I will adduce
Three powerful reasons by way of excuse:

In the first place, unless I am grossly deceived,
I myself am I in conscience the party aggrieved,
And, therefore good Sir, if a challenge *must* be,
Pray wait till that challenge be *tendered* by *me.*

Again, Sir, I think it by far the more sinful,
To stand and be shot, than to sit for a skinfull;
From whence you'll conclude (as I'd have you indeed)
That fighting composes no part of my creed—
And my courage, (which though it was never disputed,
Is not, I imagine, too, too deeply rooted)
Would prefer that its fruit, whate'er it may yield,
Should appear at *"the table,"* and not in *"the field."*

other civilized nations of antiquity.° They were never known in the British Islands till after the reign of Henry VIII. Though public combats, with permission of the court, were sometimes fought before that time.

The English borrowed the custom from the French, but it would be as ridiculous to perpetuate it, as it would to continue the tetes, systems, hoop-petticoats, and other exploded monstrosities of past ages.

If I engage in a duel the chances of escaping with my life are very few indeed. Mr. Gilchrist, a modern writer, mentions one hundred and seventy-two combats, in which sixty-three individuals were killed, and ninety-six wounded. In three of those cases both the combatants were slain, and eighteen of the survivors received the sentence of the laws which they transgressed. In what a desperate lottery then is this for a man to hazard reputation, limb, or life. Doubtless in the one hundred and seventy-

---

And lastly, *my life,* be it never forgot,
Possesses a value which *your's,*† Sir, does not;
So I mean to preserve it as long as I can,
Being justly entitled "a family *Man,*"
With three or four children, (I scarce know how many)
Whilst *you,* Sir, have not, or *ought not* to have any.

Besides, that the contest would be too unequal,
I doubt not will plainly appear by the sequel;
For, e'en *you* must acknowledge, it would not be meet
That one small "*Mann* of war" should engage a whole
   "*Fleet.*"
Andover, 20th July, 1826.

° M. Rollin says, "Neither amongst the Greeks or Romans, those conquerors of so many nations, and who certainly were very good judges of a point of honor, and perfectly understood wherein true glory consisted, was there so much as one single instance of a private duel in so many ages. This barbarous custom of cutting one another's throats, in expiating a pretended injury in the blood of one's dearest friends; this barbarous custom, I say, which now-a-days is called nobleness and greatness of soul, was unknown to those famous conquerors. 'They reserved,' says Sallust, 'their hatred and resentment for their enemies, and contended only for glory and virtue with their own countrymen."

† Mr. Fleet is a single man.

two cases to which he has alluded, many a fine young man had lost his life, and destroyed the happiness of his family, for the sake of some depraved female, or in a drunken quarrel.

As the nation's laws are open for redress, it is more imprudent to chastise, at the hazard of my life, the abuse, rudeness, or injustice of any person, let his rank or character be what it may, than it would to soil my hands by throwing dirt at ill-reared boys who had done the same to me, or to discontinue my journey on a well trained horse, for the purpose of chastising the common curs which run and bark at him upon the public roads.

If I must keep the society of fools and madmen, or of rude and ignorant persons, I should, even in charity to them, endeavour to preserve my temper. "The best revenge," says Marcus Aurelius Antonius, "is not to be like them." Contradiction, abusive words, or bad reports, which are in general the occasion of a challenge, are either merited or they are not. If deserved, I should quarrel only with myself for my own folly; I should acknowledge my fault, and carefully reform my conduct, for it is not beneath any man to confess his fault, and attempt a reparation of the injury which he occasions to the humblest fellow-creature; but to seek the life of him whom I have already injured is barbarous in the extreme.*

---

*In the cases which we have collected will be found hundreds of instances in which the ruffian who insulted or traduced, has slain the being whom he had excited. We have some, however, of a much more generous description; at present we shall only quote an anecdote of Peter Pindar.—Dr. Walcot, notwithstanding his satirical disposition, never was in more than one scrape which seriously alarmed him; it was with the late General M'Cormick. "We had passed," says Walcot, "the previous forenoon alone together, when something I said more severe than I ought to the general, roused his anger. He retorted. I was more caustic than before. He went away, and sent me a challenge for the next morning. Six o'clock was the hour fixed upon; the ground to be the Green, at Truro, which at that time was sufficiently retired. There were no seconds. The window of my room, however, commanded the Green. I had scarcely got out of bed to dress for the appointment, when pulling aside the curtains, I saw the general walking up and down on the side next the river half an hour before time. The sun was just rising cloudily, the morning bitterly cold, which, with the sight of the general's pistol and his attendance on the ground before the hour appointed, were by no means calculated

As the practise has arisen from mistaken notions of false and real honor, it may be well to consider whence true honor is derived.

It is derived from pious and patriotic actions, and is generally the sentence of the wise and virtuous, pronounced upon the citizen whose conduct squares with the laws, morals, and religion of his country. Cicero says, "It is the concurring commendation of good men, and the impartial testimony of those who judge rightly concerning what is truly virtuous." Plato says, "Honour is to search for and follow what is best, and to contrive how the worst things may be turned into good."

The Romans built the Temple of Honor within that of Virtue, to show that no person should enter the former, who had not previously passed through the latter.

Intrigue or accident may deprive a good man of his reward in this world, but after his decease the odour of his memory will be sweet, and when the intriguer shall have perished, or the accident is properly explained, his name will be venerated by future generations.

---

to strengthen my nerves. I dressed, and, while doing so, made up my mind it was great folly for two old friends to pop away each other's lives. My resolution was speedily taken. I rang for my servant girl; 'Molly, light the fire instantly, make some good toast, let the breakfast be got in a minute for two.' 'Yes Sir.' My watch was within a minute of the time. Pistol in hand, I went out the back way from my house, which opened on the green. I crossed it like a lion, and went up to M'Cormick. He looked firm, but did not speak. I did. 'Good morning t'ye, General.' The General bowed. 'This is too cold a morning for fighting.' 'There is but one alternative,' said the general distantly. 'It is what you soldiers call an apology, I suppose! My dear fellow, I would rather make twenty when I was so much in the wrong as I was yesterday; but I will only make it on one condition.' 'I cannot talk of conditions, Sir,' said the General. 'Why then I will consider the condition assented to. It is that you will come in and take a good breakfast with me now ready on the table; I am exceedingly sorry if I hurt your feelings yesterday, for I meant not to do it.' We shook hands like old friends, and soon forgot our difference over tea and toast; but I did not like the pistols and that cold morning, notwithstanding. I believe many duels might end as harmlessly, could the combatants command the field as I did from my window, and on such a cold morning too!'"

True honour has been the same in all ages, and is not dependent upon the changeable fashions or opinions of mankind.

Duelling is inconsistent with true honor, for it is opposed to the opinions of the wise and virtuous portion of mankind, as well as to the laws and religion of every state in Christendom.[*]

If indeed a man were to associate with bravoes, he might justly be apprehensive of their scorn, for refusing to fight the fellow ruffian with whom he had quarrelled, but if his predilection have been invariably for civilized society, a respectful submission to the laws and religion of his country can have no other tendency than that of increasing the general good opinion of his conduct.

Magnanimity, fidelity, justice and generosity have ever been considered as good titles to true honour. The Roman Lucretia committed an offence against purity, lest that purity should be questioned, and the duellist, to avoid the character of a coward, which only the worthless would confer, pursues the very conduct of one, by neglecting to withstand a prejudice so disgraceful to the age in which we live. The chaste Susanna nobly preferred the accusation to the commission of a crime, which would have rendered her infamous amongst her tribe and nation.

Some of the bravest officers in Christendom have set examples to those who may be placed in similar circumstances. Marshall Turenne, one of the most celebrated generals whom the world has produced, knowing that the State alone should have the direction and benefit of his valour, enclosed to his sovereign a challenge he received. And Colonel Gardiner's reply, upon a similar occasion, has conferred more honor on his name, than the taking of an hundred cities could possibly have bestowed.

> "My country claims my service, but no law
> Bids me in Folly's cause my sword to draw;
> I fear not man, nor devil, but, tho' odd,
> I'm not ashamed to own I fear my God."

---

[*] Of those laws we shall have occasion to speak in our proposal for an Anti-duelling Association.

The eulogium of both has been written by the wisest of mankind. "It is the glory of a man to pass over a transgression. He that is slow to anger is better than the mighty, and he that ruleth his spirit than he that ruleth a city." Prov. xiv. and xvi.*

Napoleon's courage I believe has never yet been questioned, yet when he received a challenge to fight a duel, he treated the communication with a good humoured reproof.

If it were even allowable to punish an aggressor, it could not be either just nor generous to visit the heaviest of all human punishments for an offence perhaps of the most trifling nature, and to take upon myself the treble office of party, judge and executioner. Surely there should be some proportion between the punishment and the crime.

If a man commit murder, his punishment is only death, and shall a life be sought in satisfaction for an offensive expression, which, perhaps, was used by a person heated with wine, or under the influence of mistake or passion.

---

*An Athenian general, having a dispute with his colleague, who was of Sparta, a man of fiery disposition, the latter lifted up his cane to strike him. The Athenian, far from resenting the outrage in what is now called a gentleman-like manner, said, "do strike if you please, *but hear me.*" He never dreamed of cutting the Lacedemonian's throat, but bore with his passionate temper as the infirmity of a friend who had a thousand good qualities to overbalance that defect.

The celebrated Henderson, the actor, was seldom known to be in a passion. When at Oxford, he was one day debating with a fellow student, who not keeping his temper, threw a glass of wine in his face. Mr. Henderson took out his handkerchief, wiped his face, and coolly said "that, sir, was a digression; now for the argument."

Sir Walter Raleigh was long celebrated as a duellist, and, after killing several of his adversaries, became so shocked at the barbarity of the custom, that he determined he would not fight another duel. Having engaged in a warm dispute with a young man at a coffee-house, the latter had the imprudence to spit in the face of the veteran, who, instead of chastising him in the usual manner with his sword, calmly took his handkerchief from his pocket, wiped his face, and said, "Could I as easily wipe the stain of killing you from my conscience, as I can this spit from my face, you should not live a moment." The youth was so forcibly struck with the dignity of Sir Walter's behaviour, that he immediately begged his pardon.

When stripes were deserved under the Mosaic law, God forbade that more than forty blows should be given to any man; and the Jews, anxious to be rather on the side of mercy, never exceeded thirty-nine; but the duellist would inflict the highest punishment upon his unfortunate antagonist, for the most trifling offence.

If rough language and ill usage be not deserved, the shame attaches only to him who has adopted them, for every person who has common sense values a man upon his personal merits, and will not condemn him because of the incivility, ill-nature, or malice of another. Neither will it be expected he should teach good manners to those who want them, as the world would afford him rather too much employment. The injured person may vindicate his character by evidence, or a statement of his case; but he cannot possibly do so by challenging the aggressor, for the guilty are always more ready to fight duels than the innocent.

Duelling is against the interests of myself, my family, my country, its morals, and religion.

I may receive a wound, which may render life a burden to me, or deprive a parent, brother, sister, wife, or child of my protection. I may grievously wound, or eternally destroy my unfortunate antagonist, and chastise his unoffending parent, wife, or child for his offence; and when in a generous moment I reflect upon the fate of my antagonist, who can afford me consolation.

History furnishes many instances, in which the seasonable energies of a single man have rescued his country from impending ruin, and perhaps I may yet live long enough to confer some benefit on mine. Had Washington or Nelson, when young, fallen a victim to this vice, how great had been the loss to America or England!

Themistocles, the great Athenian general, who was so justly called the Lover of his Country, when struck by Eurybiades in the public council, preferred the interests of the commonwealth to the indulgence of resentment; and Aristides, though banished by the Athenians through the interest of that general, being informed that the Greeks at Salamis were pressed by the Persian fleet, generously called upon Themistocles, not to upbraid him as an enemy, but to assist him with his valuable counsel for the public good, alleging that their only contention ought to be, who should render the better service to his country.

Cæsar has recorded another interesting case, in which Titus Pulfio and Lucius Varenus, two centurions of his army, had a very grievous quarrel; but, instead of seeking for revenge by duel, they strove to excel each other in acts of bravery against the Gauls, and, at periods of considerable danger, each was the saviour of the other's life.

A generous patriot sets no limit to his virtues, and will not make the example of a fellow citizen the scanty measure of his own; he will not consider that which may make him the equal of another, but what may make him great and generous beyond all precedent.

The conduct of an individual has an influence upon the morals of his nation, and as I respect those morals, I should not inflict a wound upon them by my own example.

But if duelling is offensive to common sense, the interests of myself, my family, my country, and its morals,—how much more offensive must it be before the holy Author of my existence, into whose sacred presence I would rashly rush.

He who kills another offers violence to the Almighty, robs him of his image, destroys his work, and lessens the honor paid him. Murder was the first offence forbidden, when the seven precepts were given to Noah, with a solemn injunction respecting their careful transmission to that patriarch's posterity; its prohibition has frequently been repeated, and all actions which led to its commission were declared crimes, subject to the infliction of punishment, by the Mosaic law. Murder is sacrilege of the very highest nature, for man has been described as the temple of his God. It is called a crying sin, because it calls to Heaven for vengeance. Such strange and miraculous discoveries of blood have taken place, that it is evident "Murder, though it have no tongue, will speak with most miraculous organ."

"Surely the blood of your lives will I require," saith the Lord, "at the hand of every man's brother will I require the life of man; whoso sheddeth man's blood, by man shall his blood be shed, for in the image of God created he man."

There was no sacrifice appointed for it, as for other sins; neither was there any sanctuary nor place of refuge to which the murderer might flee. Even Moses or Joshua had not authority to pardon it, or to dispense with any portion of the prescribed chastisement, as all recompense or satisfaction for the life of a murderer was forbidden by the Lord. Num. xxxv. 31. Lest the magistrate should neglect to enforce the punishment, it was declared that the land could not be cleansed from blood, but by the blood of him by whom it had been shed. When one was slain, the adjoining city was to make a solemn purgation. No killing was justified except, First, by order of the magistrate, after an impartial trial; Second, in war; and, Third, in one's own and necessary defence. Three years of famine were endured in the time of David, for the blood of the Gibeonites, which his predecessor had unjustly shed, and the scourge was not removed until seven of Saul's offspring were executed for his crime.

David was forbidden to build the temple of Jerusalem, because he was a man of blood; and Jacob cursed the cruel wrath of his own sons, Levi and Simeon, because in their anger they had slain a man.

Philo says, "If any should set upon another with his sword, intending to kill him, he is guilty of murder, though he do not succeed; nor will it excuse him that his attempt was frustrated, and therefore he deservedly suffereth the same punishment. So, if any who dare not make an open attack, shall lie in wait and deceitfully work the death of another, he is an execrable villain, polluted in his mind; for as we count not only them enemies, who fight us actually by armies on land, and by navies at sea, but also all those who make their offensive preparations, and who advance their warlike engines before our gates and walls, though as yet no formal attack has been made,—so they not only ought to be accounted murderers who actually kill, but those also who do all that in them lies secretly or openly to take away the life of another, though their attempt should fail."

If I fight a duel, I shall violate those vows which were made for me in baptism, that I should renounce the devil and his works, with the pomps and vanities of a corrupted world; I shall offend against that Gospel which forbids revenge, which strenuously enforces the forgiveness of all injuries, and even the return of benevolent for evil actions; which so forcibly enjoins gentleness, which tells me that fighting is a produce of our lusts, and that the devil was a murderer from the beginning; which, lest I should give place to him, recommends me not to let the sun go down upon my anger, and which commands me as much as in me lies to live in peace with all men.

Every argument which can be adduced against war or suicide is applicable to the crime of duelling; and shall I, through a weak compliance with a vicious custom, do wanton injury to my adversary, my friends, my body, and my soul,—to my country, its morality, its religion, and its God? Forbid it, gracious Heaven! forbid it, love of country! forbid it, human reason! More real honor may be gained by withstanding this vile practice once, than by slaying one hundred adversaries in as many combats, and while all the wise and pious are of this opinion, I will fearlessly follow the examples of the brave Turenne and Gardiner. I will cautiously avoid the society of those who use provoking language or behaviour, and I will use my best endeavours to promote the establishment of a Court of Honor, and of an Antiduelling Society, like that which has already been established in New York.

JOSEPH HAMILTON.

ANNADALE COTTAGE,
    NEAR DUBLIN.

THE COURT OF HONOR
CIRCULAR

"But those
Stand at another Bar than that of Law."

———,

Should you approve of the accompanying "Extract from the Dublin Freeman's Journal," I shall feel obliged by your benevolent co-operation in the achievement of its object, with Noblemen, Officers, and others, of unquestionable bravery, who are less hostile to the principle, than to the abuse of duelling.

There are many honorable men, who with Laertes say,

"I will no reconcilement,
Till by some older masters of known honor,
I have a voice and precedent of peace,
To keep my name ungored."

Let rank and influence combine with promptitude, in effecting a great moral revolution. The coeuvrechief of chivalry, softened down the rigors of the tournament, and the knights of Malta fought their duels under saving regulations.° Who then can be an advocate for unnecessary slaughter, and hold an envi-

---

°Rene d'Anjou, who wrote upon the forms of tournaments, informs us that before the conflict was commenced, the king of arms used to lead some valiant knight or squire before the women, and say, "Thrice noble and redoubted knight, or thrice noble and gentle squire, as it is always the custom of women to have a compassionate heart, those who are assembled in this company, in order to behold the tournament which is to be held to-morrow, make known their pleasure that the combat before their eyes must not be too violent, or so

able station amongst civilized society? If prohibited to bathe in royal reservoirs of honor, he may skulk with unraised vizor, and polluted plume, to herd with tiplers at a tavern, or with blustering bullies at a brothel; but he can no longer with impunity occasion such a scene as we have sketched for our reflections upon duelling, and under which we might have quoted those sad lines from Hervey.

"Here lies the grief of a fond mother, and the blasted expectation of an indulgent father. The youth grew up like a well-watered plant; he shot deep, and rose high; but just as the cedar began to tower, and promised, ere long, to be the pride of the wood, and prince among the neighbouring trees—behold! the axe is laid unto the root; the fatal blow is struck; and all its branching honors tumbled to the dust. And did he fall alone? No; the hopes of his father that begat him, and the pleasing prospects of her that bare him, fell, and were crushed together with him."

When parties wishing for the opinion of a Court of Honor, may feel a delicacy in the publication of their names, which might, by possibility, occasion their being held to bail, their cases may be anonymously, or confidentially communicated to the Registrar, who can assemble a Court in London, or in Dublin, at a very few days notice.

By favouring me with the name of any nobleman or gentle-

---

ordered that they cannot bear assistance in time of need. Therefore they command the most renowned knight or squire of the assembly, whoever he may be, to bear right to-morrow, on the end of a lance, this present coeuvrechief, in order that when any one should be too grievously pressed, he may lower this coeuvrechief over the crest of those who attack him, who must immediately cease to strike, and not dare to touch their adversary any more; for from this hour, during the rest of that day, the women take him under their protection and safeguard." The coeuvrechief, which was a kind of hood enriched with embroidery, was then entrusted to his care. The knights of Malta were restrained to fight their duels in a particular street, where ladies, knights, and priests, were generally found to exercise their privilege, and say with Randolf,

"Hold! I command you both."

man who may be willing to assist me, or the particulars of any case, possessed of remarkable or interesting features, you will considerably enhance the value of your kindness.

Any franked communication may be forwarded to my residence, or to the London Coffee-House, on Ludgate-hill, for

Your most obedient, and
Very humble servant,
JOSEPH HAMILTON.

Annadale Cottage,
   Dublin.

Extract from the Freeman's Journal of July 18, 1828.

"IN several of the continental states, Courts of Honor have been established lately, for the adjustment of such differences as might lead to duels. The Kings of Prussia* and Bavaria, are amongst the number of their patrons, and the late Duke of York was favourable to their institution in Great Britain. The time has passed away when Duelling was resorted to for pastime, or the love of fighting, and men meet now upon affairs of honor, for no other reason under heaven, but because they think the world requires that they should fight. Let them but feel, that they have fully satisfied the wishes of mankind, and they will avail themselves of every honorable source of reconciliation. Thus, in the army, where the highest tone of chivalry may be reasonably sought for, it is customary for a gentleman to abide by the opinion of his brother officers.

"Mr. JOSEPH HAMILTON, of Annadale Cottage, near Dublin, who was the author of two works on Duelling, is now collecting

---

*The King of Prussia has addressed a Cabinet order to the Minister of War, enjoining him to signify to the army his majesty's displeasure at the frequency of duels, which originating in miserable trifles, have deprived the country of many promising officers, and plunged their families into mourning. His majesty's orders are, that the corps of officers and generals shall, by vigilance and exhortation, combat this fatal prejudice, and, in case of need, bring those who are the authors of the challenge before the tribunals of honor, according to the ordinance of 15th February, 1821.

the names of persons, whose station in society, or experience, either as Principals or Seconds, should qualify them to form a competent tribunal, for the decision of all questions on the point of honor; and until some other gentleman shall be kind enough to occupy his place, he has volunteered to be the Registrar. He proposes that the court shall be composed of a president, four vice-presidents, and such persons of the following description as may avow their readiness to act on such a tribunal; videlicet, peers, the sons of peers, members of parliament, baronets, knights, the honorable society of King's Inns, the military, naval, medical, and surgical professions, gentlemen who have filled the offices of mayor or High Sheriff, justices of the peace, estated gentlemen, members of the law, jockey, and ouzel galley clubs, bankers, bank directors, and merchants, with authors, proprietors, and editors of all public works. That a member of the royal family shall be respectfully solicited to patronize the effort. That principals, their friends, and every individual of the court, shall be at liberty to put any question in writing, on which it may be desirable to take a judgment, and that the *ayes* and *noes* shall only be expressed by white or black beans, to prevent the possibility of jealousy between the suitors and their judges.—He proposes, that the latter shall be assembled by the registrar, if in the capital, or by a member of the court, if in the country, at the request of either a principal or second. To prevent the evils which frequently arise from personal collision, and from oral statements, he proposes that all facts and arguments shall be submitted to the court in writing, and upon the honor of the parties.—The expenses of the establishment to be defrayed by the parties, and by the voluntary contributions of benevolent individuals.

"Such a court, in every city, shire, and country town, throughout the empire, might prevent a number of fatal duels, arising out of very trifling causes; and, doubtless, would experience adequate support from the truly sensible and brave. Mr. Hamilton has collected nearly one thousand accounts of remarkable quarrels, challenges, replies, duels, rencontres, apologies, and reconciliations, which must be highly useful to refer to as precedents, and from which he derived considerable aid, in the formation of the Royal Code of Honor—a work which was submitted to all the European sovereigns; which obtained the thanks of the Duke of York, and which Sir Walter Scott considered as 'highly capable of softening the atrocities of our Gothic custom.'"

We now most respectfully solicit the prompt and generous co-operation of every individual in society.° We beseech the mothers, sisters, wives, and daughters of the world, to banish from their circles the habitual duellist,

> "Who kills his man, and triumphs o'er his maid."

But chiefly we implore the aid of those in power; The Royal Fountains of all worldly honors, to justify our hopes, to crown our labours, and to draw down heavenly benedictions on their thrones.

°Prince Eugene said to Zindendorf, "The soldier is so weary of being cruel during war, that he ceases to be so in the time of peace. I wish that every minister who decides between them, had been in the service, that he might know what it is. He would consent to arbitrations, as in a lawsuit, mediations, moderations, before he would determine to spill so much blood."

BRIEF

ANECDOTES OF DUELLING

"Nothing extenuate;
Nor set down aught in malice."

We shall commence our collection of Anecdotes and Cases,[*] with the following letter, from a highly-gifted gentleman, because it may induce the transmission of other documents in time for our intended supplement.

Dear Sir—When I had the pleasure of meeting you at the house of my friend, Mr. Gartlan, you made a request that I would furnish you with a statement of the particulars of the remarkable duel, between Mr. Price, brother to the present manager of Drury-lane theatre, and a Major Green, of the British army, which took place near Hoboken, on the Jersey shore, opposite to the city of New York:—absence from home, and some pressing affairs, have prevented me from laying them sooner before you.

That fatal meeting took place in the spring of 1816, and being in the city of New York at the time, I can only trace its origin from a recollection of the statement then current in that city. Major Green arrived at New York in the winter preceding, on his way to Canada, it being the usual route when the St. Laurence is frozen. During his stay there he went to the theatre, and took a position in a box next to one occupied by some

---

[*]Although we do not like the style in which many of our Anecdotes and Documents is written, yet we prefer it to an altered one, which might by possibility have influence on points of such a very delicate description.

American ladies, who were escorted by Mr. Price, whose brother was manager to the theatre. In the course of the entertainment Mr. Price complained to Major Green of what he conceived to be an insulting liberty he had taken in staring rather too steadfastly at some of the ladies under his protection. Major Green in apology stated, that he was a stranger just arrived from Europe, that he was ignorant of the manners of America, and that in looking at the fair women in his box, he only exercised a privilege common to every man in England, of regarding beauty in whatever place or rank it was to be found. If, said he, that privilege be not allowed here, and that I have offended by exercising it, I beg pardon for having unintentionally given an offence. The matter so far ended. Major Green pursued his route to head-quarters in Canada, but he was not long there, when some person communicated to him, that after his departure from New York, Mr. Price boasted he had made a British officer knuckle to him, and he had taught him manners,—with some other observations reflecting on his honor and courage. These remarks being generally known, the Major felt himself bound to notice them. He laid the case before the commander and officers of his corps, who declared he was bound to seek an explanation; and accordingly got leave to proceed to New York when the rigours of winter had passed over.—He waited on Mr. Price, and demanded if he had made the observations alluded to. He did not deny them, and being asked for an apology, would give none; so that a meeting became inevitable.

By the laws of New York, duelling is so far repressed, as to punish the survivor with death, as if he were guilty of murder. To evade them, cases arising in the city of New York are generally decided on the opposite shore of the Hudson, which divides New York from the state of Jersey, where the laws against duelling are not so severe. The spot usually selected is near Hoboken, being a piece of ground of two or three perches square, on the rocky and precipitous bank of the river; it is only accessible by water, and a more retired or silent situation for the murderous operation of the laws of honor could not be found.

It was on a sabbath day the parties took boat at New York, and met on this fatal ground—the only spot in the world, perhaps, which is exclusively used as a field of honor. The parties tossed for ground, when Major Green obtained the south side, and Mr. Price the north. The distance was twelve paces, and the parties fired together by word. The first fire was ineffectual, when some effort was used by Major Green's second for an adjustment, without effect. The second fire was alike ineffectual. Major Green and his second then stated, they were unwilling to carry the matter further. Major Green had no personal hostility to Mr. Price; the courage of the parties had been sufficiently attested, and the Major having vindicated his honor, so far as to preserve his reputation amongst his brother officers, was ready to walk off the ground. To this Mr. Price objected; and according to the unfortunate and sanguinary practice in America, insisted on continuing the fire until either fell. "If murder then," said Major Green, "and not a vindication of character, be the object, I must consult my safety—let us advance three paces." It was agreed: the distance was thus reduced to six paces—the word was given,—Mr. P. received his antagonist's ball through the brain, and fell dead upon the spot.

After this calamitous affair, Major Green immediately departed; and to avoid all trouble, went on board a ship, then under weigh for Europe. The news of this duel was not generally known in the city until next morning, when it produced a painful excitement, Mr. Price being highly esteemed through an extensive circle of acquaintance.

Thus far this unfortunate affair: but as you are writing on the subject of duelling, I will add a few circumstances that may prove interesting to you. It was in this place, the only son of General Hamilton fell in a duel, which sad event induced the General to write a work against the practice of duelling, which attests the force of his Christian-like and philosophic mind. But such is often the force of circumstances, that public men cannot control their actions, and the General lost his life on the same fatal ground on which his son expired. A difference arose between him and a Mr. Aaron Burr, a lawyer of New York, who was then candidate for the high office of Vice President of the United States, on the democratic interest; the General was the great leader of the federal interest. From the rancour and vehemence of party feeling at that time, a reconciliation could not be effected, and the fatal extremity was resorted to. By his death, the public mind in America received a shock, co-equal with the gratitude due to him for the eminent services he had rendered his country. He was the friend of Washington, and chiefly contributed to the formation of the federal constitution of the United States, in 1787. His remains were interred with all due honors, in the principal episcopal church of the city, where a splendid monument has been erected to his memory.

On the morning after the death of Mr. Price, a friend of mine, from Bridgetown, Barbadoes, who was afterwards killed in a duel there, proposed to me, that we should take a boat, and visit the place where these, and so many other duels had taken place. It is about four miles from New York; but before we went there, my friend proposed to me the opportunity of seeing the ex-Vice President, Mr. Burr, with whom he had some professional business as a lawyer. The office was crowded with persons; and while my friend was engaged in conversation, I attentively viewed his person. His emaciated and care-worn figure, fortified my conviction that, to a sensitive mind, to be the survivor in a duel is nearly as disastrous as death itself.

We entered our boat, and directed our course for the nearest habitation to the duelling ground, to which the boatmen generally retire while the affair is going on. We there took in a person, who narrated the circumstances of the last and many preceding duels; one of which had occurred a short time before, when the parties fought by moonlight, and fired nine rounds.—On reaching the spot, the ground was stained with gore, and we picked up a ball from the turf beneath where Mr. Price had stood. A white marble monument has been erected here, also, to the memory of the lamented General Hamilton, with a suitable inscription.

In your work on duelling, you recommend that the seconds should never place the antagonists near a rock, a wall, or a hedge, or any object running parallel to the parties, as it gives an undue advantage to one over the other, by rendering the aim more certain. The truth of this has often been exemplified on the duelling ground I have described. Before the erection of the monument to General Hamilton, the rock served as a direction to the person on the south side, while the person on the north had his face to the water, and it is remarkable, that the deaths of the three persons I have mentioned, occurred on the same side, that is, the north. At present, the monument is in front of the rock, but its base being long, it serves as a direction.

I find these details have carried me to a greater length than I expected:—in the hope that your benevolent labors may tend to check a practice that has descended to us from barbarous times, and equally violates human and divine law, I have the honor to be,

Dear Sir,

Your most obedient servant,

THOMAS BRODIGAN.

In justice to the memory of Mr. Price, we insert another account of the same transaction, which we received from our worthy friend, Counsellor Dillon, who happened to be at New York at the period of the duel.

"Mr. Price espoused the cause of a young lady, who had been insulted at the New York theatre. The British officer, sensible of his error, made a very ingenuous apology; but on his return to Montreal, his head quarters, he was put into Coventry by his brother officers, on a charge of having apologized to a person whom they called a *damned Yankee,* which they considered beneath the dignity of a British officer. He was obliged to return accompanied by some of his brother officers; he publicly struck Mr. Price in Broadway, which led to a meeting at Hoboken, on the opposite shore of the Hudson River, at twelve yards distance with pistols, in a valley between two great rocks. Each fired six shots; no apology would be made; and the seventh shot entered the head of Mr. Price, who died immediately. The public feeling was evinced by a splendid marble monument upon the scene of action, in testimony of respect for him while living, and regret for his fall in such a sanguinary conflict."

ROYAL AND
VICEREGAL QUARRELS

"I set so low a price upon my blood,
That you may tap my veins at your good pleasure."

CYRUS AND THE KING OF ASSYRIA.

When Cyrus drew nigh to Babylon, he sent a challenge to the King of Assyria, offering to decide their quarrel by a single combat; but his challenge was not accepted of.

DAVID AND GOLIA[T]H.

David, who was afterwards exalted to the throne of Israel, accepted of a challenge which had frequently been published by Golia[t]h. They met in a plain between the Philistine and Hebrew armies, and David slew his adversary.

TURNUS AND ÆNEAS.

These two princes fought in single combat, which proved fatal to the former.

ARUNS AND BRUTUS.

After Tarquin's expulsion from the throne, and when he was preparing to engage the army of the republic, commanded by Valerius and Brutus, his son Aruns, seeing the latter at a distance, singled him out for combat: they both met with such rage, that eager only to assail, and thoughtless of defending, they both fell dead upon the field together.

ANTONY AND CÆSAR.

Antony having challenged Augustus Cæsar to fight a duel, the latter very calmly replied, "if Antony is weary of his life, tell him there are other ways to death than the point of my sword."

The Hebrew and Roman duels were all fought on public grounds. History furnishes us with no examples of duels which arose from private quarrels.

HENRY IV.

Henry Plantagenet or Bolingbroke, who was afterwards King of England, challenged the Duke of Norfolk, and when due preparation was made for the combat, they were interrupted by the Ho! Ho! of a herald, at the king's command.

HENRY V.

When Prince of Wales, struck Judge Gascoyne while presiding on the bench. That independent functionary sent the wayward Prince to prison; yet upon his exaltation to the British throne, Henry lost no opportunity of evincing his concern for the outrage, or his respect for the Chief Justice.

TWO IRISH PRINCES.

One Irish provincial prince sent the following laconic message to another: "Pay me your tribute, or else—" To which the other replied, "I owe you no tribute; and if I did—"

MALCOLM III. KING OF SCOTLAND.

The King having received information that one of his nobles had conspired against his life, enjoined the strictest silence on the part of the informer, and took no notice of it himself, until the person who was accused of the treason came to court, for the purpose of executing his design. The next morning, the king went out to hunt, with all his courtiers, and when they were in the centre of a forest, he drew the traitor aside, where unattended, he addressed him thus: "Behold, we are here alone, armed and mounted equally. Nobody hears or sees us, or can give either of us help against the other. If, then, you are a brave man, perform your purpose, accomplish the promise which you made my enemies.—If you think I should be killed by you, when can you do it better? when more opportunely? when more manly? Have you prepared poison for me?—that is a womanish treason. Or would you murder me in my bed?—an adulteress could do that. Or have you concealed a dagger to stab me secretly?—that is the deed of a ruffian. Rather act like a soldier, act like a man, and fight with me hand to hand, that your treason may, at least, be free from baseness." The traitor fell at his feet, and implored a pardon which was granted.

FRANCIS I. AND CHARLES V.

At the breaking up of a treaty, in the year 1527, between the Emperor Charles V. and Francis I., the former desired the Herald of Francis to acquaint his Sovereign, that he would henceforth, consider him not only as a base violator of public faith, but as a stranger to the honor and integrity becoming a gentleman.—Francis, instantly sent back the Herald with a defiance, giving Charles the *lie* in form, and challenging him to single combat, with any weapon he might chuse. The challenge was at once accepted, both were equally brave, and though all thoughts of so extraordinary a duel, were at last, laid aside, the example of such illustrious personages, (so powerful is the dominion of fashion) produced instantaneous and melancholy effects throughout all Europe.

GUSTAVUS ADOLPHUS.

Gustavus Adolphus, at one of his public reviews, having a dispute with Colonel Seaton, an officer in his service, gave him a blow, which he resented highly. As soon as the review was over, the Colonel repaired to the King's apartment, and demanded his discharge; which his majesty signed, and the Colonel withdrew without a word being said upon the subject of the quarrel.

Gustavus, however, on coolly considering the matter, reproached himself for his want of temper, and hearing that Seaton intended to set out next day for Denmark, he followed him, attended by an officer and two or three grooms. When his majesty reached the Danish frontier, he left all his attendants except one, and overtaking Seaton on a large plain, he said to him "Dismount, sir; that you have been injured I acknowledge, and I am now come to give you the satisfaction of a gentleman, for being now out of my own dominions, Gustavus and you are equal. We have both I see swords and pistols; alight immediately, and receive that satisfaction which your wounded honor demands." Seaton recovering from his surprise, dismounted, as the king had already done, and falling to his knees, said,—"Sire you have more than given me satisfaction, by making me your equal. God forbid that my sword should do any mischief to so brave and gracious a prince. Permit me to return to Stockholm, and allow me the honor to live and die in your service." The king raised him from the ground, embraced him, and they returned together to Stockholm.

PETER THE GREAT.

Peter the Great was in conversation with Admiral Apraxin, when the Vice Admiral, Senavin, presented him with a salver of wine; the emperor impatiently threw back his arm, overset the salver, struck the vice admiral, and pursued his discourse as if nothing had occurred. Afterwards, recollecting himself, he asked Apraxin if he had not struck some person: "Yes," said he, "your majesty has struck the vice admiral, Senavin: it is true, he was in the wrong for interrupting your majesty, but he is a very honest man, and a brave officer." Peter then reproached himself for striking an officer of that rank; sent for him immediately, begged his pardon, kissed him, and sent him a valuable present.

THE DUKE OF YORK.

This case, which we reserve for the Military and Naval Duels, was the first in which a prince of the blood, in England, was challenged by a subject; but

THE PRINCE DE CONDE,

a few years before, met an officer of his own regiment. The Prince, in a violent passion, gave the officer a blow: he sold out, followed the prince every where, and on all occasions, public or private, was constantly in his view. The prince took the alarm, apprehending that the officer intended to assassinate him: he accordingly asked him, what were his wishes and intentions. "I have a claim to reparation for my injured honor," said the officer. "I will give it to you," replied the prince: "follow me." The swords were drawn and measured—the officer touched that of his adversary, and instantly dropped his own. "My Prince," said he, "you have condescended to fight me, and it is enough. I am satisfied. The blow you gave me no longer rankles in my breast. It is fully expiated." The Prince of Conde, to mark the high sense he entertained of the officer's conduct, restored him to his situation, and speedily promoted him.

THE PRESENT KING OF FRANCE AND DUKE DE BOURBON.

The present King of France, when Comte d'Artois, fought the Duke de Bourbon. The Comte de Nivages was second to the latter, and M. de Crussal to the former. The quarrel originated at a masqued ball. They long fought, with swords; but the Comte d'Artois growing impatient, pushed his adversary with such vigor, that he wounded him in the arm; when the seconds interfered successfully, and effected a reconciliation.

NAPOLEON.

It is said that the brave Sir Sidney Smith, during the siege of Acre, sent a message to Napoleon, who replied, that if the gallant knight wished to amuse himself, he would chalk out a few yards of neutral ground, and send him a grenadier, whose size should encrease the chance of being hit, and that if Sir Sidney shot his representative, the victory should be acknowledged by himself; but he had at that time too much business upon his hands, in directing the physical energies of his country, to indulge in the amusements of a school-boy with an English Commodore.

The following according to Captain Medwin's statement is Napoleon's own account of the transaction.

"When the French Army was before St. Jean d'Acre, he (Sir Sidney), had a paper privately distributed among the officers and soldiers, tending to induce them to revolt and quit me;

on which I issued a proclamation, denouncing the English Commanding Officer as a madman and prohibiting all intercourse with him. This nettled Sir Sidney so much, that he sent me a challenge to meet him in single combat on the beach of Caiffa. My reply was, that when Marlborough appeared for that purpose, I should be at his service; but I had other duties to fulfil, besides fighting a duel with an English Commodore."

THE LATE HEREDITARY PRINCE OF HESSE HOMBURGH.

After his marriage with the Princess Elizabeth, his serene highness was involved in an affair of honor, on which occasion Prince Esterhazy acted as his second, and the reparation which he sought for was obtained.

We had the honor of a personal acquaintance with his highness, whose hospitality we have shared, and we believe he was as brave and honorable a soldier as the world could produce.

THE VICEROY OF NORWAY.

At a dinner given in Christiana, by Count de Sandels, the Viceroy of Norway, to a party of gentlemen, who were governors of Swedish provinces, he insulted his company; and received nine messages next day.

THE LORD LIEUTENANT OF IRELAND.

Lord Townsend, on retiring from the government of Ireland, fought and wounded the Earl of Bellamont.

We speak advisedly when we assert, that in general, the sovereigns of Christendom deplore the existence of a practice which has deprived them of brave officers, and of useful subjects; a practice with they think might be advantageously put an end to; and which must yield to one united effort of benevolence and power. We shall therefore look with great anxiety to the proceedings of the next general Congress, should no earlier arrangement be adopted through the embassys in Paris, or in London.

DANGER OF BEING SECONDS,
OR BY-STANDERS

"They who with quarrels interpose,
Must often wipe a bloody nose."

The man who acts as second, always runs the hazard of becoming a principal himself.

When Major Pack and Mr. Matthew were engaged at a tavern in Dublin, Mr. Macnamara, the second to the latter, having secured the door and drawn his sword, declared that in affairs of this description it was inconvenient to remain a cool spectator, and with Captain Creed's permission, he would have the honor of entertaining him in the same manner. The four fought until Pack and Creed fell, covered with wounds of the most desperate description.

In Mr. Deerhurst's description of the fatal duel between the Duke of B—— and Lord B——, it is stated, that "a little pause having intervened in the work of death, his Grace's second proposed a reconciliation, but that the ardent thirst for each other's blood so overpowered the strongest arguments of reason, they insisted on executing each other's will, whatever might be the consequence. Nay, the anger of his Grace was raised to such a height of revenge, that he swore, if for the future either of the seconds interfered, he would make his way through his body."

Mr. Edward Hickman, of hospitable, chivalrous, and facetious notoriety, both in Clare and Dublin, informed us, that he was once placed in a very awkward situation, as the second to a gentleman, who could not be prevailed upon to quit the carriage on its arrival at the ground.—Mr. H. offered to supply the situation of his principal, but received a generous dispensation from the service, with an offer of seats in the carriage and at the breakfast table of the adverse party, which he accepted; leaving his principal, who was overcome by religious or parental feeling, to return by himself to the place from whence he came.

Mr. Cæsar Colclough was second to a gentleman, who was not punctual in his attendance on the ground. The opposite party began to rail at this conduct, until Mr. Colclough assured them, that they should not lose their morning's amusement, as he was prepared to stand in the place of the absent gentleman himself. This alternative, however, was not necessary, as his friend appeared soon after, and received an apology for the offence which had occasioned the appointment. In this case, both the parties left the ground in great good humour.

Captain S—— found it necessary to take such strong precautions against the elopement of a principal, for whom he stood committed as a second, that his life was attempted as he lay in bed, which induced him to shoot his prisoner, through certain large and fleshy muscles situated in his rear.

In the case of Maher and Grady, Mr. Maher's second informed the celebrated Edward Lysaght, who was the second to Mr. Grady, that his pistol was cocked. Ned who, as Sir Jonah Barrington observes, was ever ready at a joke, a bottle, or a pistol, replied with promptitude, "Well, then, do you cock yours, and let us take a slap ourselves, as we are idle."

The Tipperary Code directed the seconds how they were to fight with swords, and how with pistols.—When Mr. John Bourke fought Mr. Bodkin, near Glinsk, the seconds also fought. The four gentlemen amused themselves at right angles, upon a signal shot being fired by an attending umpire.

Nothing is more difficult, than for seconds to divest themselves of partiality for their principals; to agree in their opinions of the case; or their description of its management and issue. The most trifling feature in a verbal or written statement of the transaction, may involve either of them in a serious quarrel with more individuals than one. In the case of Messrs. Peele and O'Connell, the seconds, Sir Charles Saxton and George Lidwell, Esq. having differed respecting the published statement of the case, became involved as principals themselves.

A meeting took place in January, 1818, between Mr.

O'Callaghan and Lieutenant Bailey, late of the 58th regiment. The parties had been seconds to two other gentlemen, who, owing to some accident, neglected to meet, and were posted as cowards by the respective seconds. When the seconds met, they mutually preferred charges of avoiding the appointment, and became principals themselves, near Primrose-hill.—After two shots on each side, Lieutenant Bailey received a fatal wound, and fell. Mr. O'Callaghan and the two seconds paid the most humane attention to Mr. Bailey, who frequently shook hands with them, and acknowledged they had acted honorably towards him. Bailey died, the other parties were tried, convicted of manslaughter, and imprisoned for three months.

The Dublin Morning Post of November 29, 1823, mentions a duel, in which a second exposed himself to the hazard of becoming a principal, and to the animadversions of the public, by defeating an overture for reconciliation, with the curt remark, that the parties came to the ground not to talk but to fight.

The same journal stated, on the 8th of November, 1828; that at a meeting near Dolly-Mount, between Messrs. L——ft——e and M'G——ty, some unpleasant difference between the seconds was the cause of another duel before the parties left the ground.

A duel was fought between two gentlemen on Bagshot Heath, which proved fatal to one of the seconds, in consequence of his standing too near his man; he was shot in the left side, and died in two hours.

In a case at Boulogne, between two boys, one of the seconds was dangerously wounded. In another case, between two privates, a Frenchman and an Italian, who fought with muskets, and were *blindfolded,* the seconds were in very great danger of being shot.

The celebrated Jemmy Keough, who "did not like to see any body fight but himself and his opponent," unfortunately shot a cripple in the Phoenix Park.

In the fatal case of Camelford and Best, his Lordship governed all the conduct of his second and himself with the most erroneous and despotic spirit.

The friends of General Mason were very blameable for submitting to the dictatorial spirit of his instructions, which we shall publish in their proper place; and the friend of Mr. Paul, when he fought Sir Francis Burdett, might justly be included in the censure.

Mr. M'Donough from the neighbourhood of Portumna, in the country of Galway, was tried at the spring assizes of 1829, in Philipstown, for the murder of a Mr. Davis, under the following circumstances:—A Mr. Sadlier and a Mr. Dowling quarrelled and a duel was the consequence. Davis was second to Sadlier and M'Donough to Dowling, who was his uncle. The principals exchanged shots, and were removed from the ground without any explanation or apology on either side. Davis being dissatisfied challenged the other second, which M'Donough declined on the ground that he had no quarrel with Davis. "You sha'nt have that to say," observed the other, and spat in his face. M'Donough nothing moved by this outrageous conduct, took out his handkerchief and wiped his face, declaring that he would resent the insult in a more proper place. Davis however, insisted that he should fight him without stirring from the spot on which he stood, and threw one end of his handkerchief at him in token of defiance. Irritated by repeated provocations the prisoner drew forth a pistol, and shot him through the head. The ball unfortunately passed afterwards through the body of a country man who also lost his life. M'Donough with great difficulty mounted his horse and escaped from a mob, who were the partizans of Davis. The jury acquitted the prisoner, to the great satisfaction of a crowded court, who were aware that he was a gentleman of excellent character and most unoffending demeanour.

In Ireland, a second agreed a few years since, that the principals should leave the ground after receiving and escaping each other's fire several times; but protested against their shaking hands,— which induced one of the principals to say, that the other had a scoundrel for his adviser. This immediately brought on a second duel, in which a pocket-handkerchief measured the distance, until one of the parties fell, never to behold his friends again.

Of this unfortunate duel (between Gillespie and William Barrington,) Sir Jonah Barrington has given the following description; and if it contain a feature of injustice to the late General Gillespie, we shall be happy to correct it in a future edition.

"William Barrington had passed his twentieth year, and had

intended without delay to embrace the military profession. He was active, lively, full of spirit and animal courage; his prominent traits were excessive good nature, and a most zealous attachment to the honor and individuals of his family.

"Gillespie, then captain in a cavalry regiment, had shortly before the period in question married a Miss Taylor, an intimate friend of ours, and was quartered in Athy, where my mother resided.

"A very close and daily intercourse sprang up between the families. After dinner, one day, at Gillespie's house, when every gentleman had taken more wine than was prudent, a dispute arose between my brother and a Mr. M'Kenzie, lieutenant in an infantry regiment quartered at the same place. The dispute never should have been suffered to arise; and as it was totally private, should, at least, never have proceeded further. But no attempt was made either to reconcile or check it, on the part of Captain Gillespie, although the thing occurred at his own table.

"Midway between Athy and Carlow was agreed on for a meeting. A crowd, as usual, attended the combat. Several gentlemen, and some relations of mine, were, I regret to say, present. In a small verdant field on the bank of the Barrow, my brother and Mr. M'Kenzie were placed. Gillespie, who had been considered as the friend and intimate of my family, *volunteered* as second to M'Kenzie, (a comparative stranger,) who was in no way averse to an amicable arrangement. Gillespie, however, would hear of none; the honor of a military man, he said, must be satisfied, and nothing but *blood,* or at least every effort to draw it, could form that satisfaction.

"The combatants fired and missed:—they fired again; no mischief was the consequence. A reconciliation was now proposed, but objected to by Gillespie: and will it be believed that, in a civilized country, when both combatants were satisfied, one of the principals should be instantly slain by a *second?* Yet such was the case: my brother stood two fires from his opponent, and whilst professing his readiness to be reconciled, was shot dead by the hand of his opponent's second.

"Gillespie himself is now departed: he died the same death that he had inflicted. But he was more favoured by Providence;—he died the death of a soldier;—he fell by the hand of the enemy, not by the weapon of an intimate.

"The principal facts proved for the prosecution were:—that after M'Kenzie and my brother had fired four shots without effect, the latter said he hoped enough had been done for both their honours, at the same time holding out his hand to M'Kenzie,—whose second, Captain Gillespie, exclaimed, that his friend *should not* be satisfied, and that the affair should proceed. The spectators combined in considering it concluded, and a small circle having been formed, my brother, who persisted in uttering his pacific wishes, interposed some harsh expressions towards Gillespie, who thereupon losing all control over his temper, suddenly threw a handkerchief to William Barrington, asking if he dared to take a corner of that. The unfortunate boy full of spirit and intrepidity, snatched at the handkerchief, and at the same moment received a ball from Gillespie, through his body—so close were they together, that his coat appeared scorched by the powder. He fell, and was carried to a cabin hard by, where he expired in great agony the same evening. As he was in the act of falling, his pistol went off. Gillespie immediately fled, and was followed by three of his own dragoons, whom he had brought with him, and who were present at the transaction, but who he declined examining upon the trial. The spectators were very numerous, and scarcely a dry eye left the field.

"Capt. Gillespie's defence rested upon an assertion on his part of irritating expressions having been used by my brother, adding that the cock of his own pistol was knocked off by my brother's fire. But that very fact proved every thing against him; because his shot *must* have been fired and have taken effect in my brother's body previously—for if the cock had been broken in the first place, Gillespie's pistol could not have gone off. In truth, the whole circumstance of a second killing a principal because he desired reconciliation was, and remains, totally unexampled in the history of duelling even in the most barbarous eras and countries.

"Judge Bradstreet, who tried the prisoners, held it to be clearly murder by law. A verdict of even manslaughter must (he contended) be returned by a forced or rather false construction;—but *acquit* him (Gillespie) generally, the jury could not.

"The prosecution was not followed up against M'Kenzie, whose conduct throughout had been that of an officer and a gentleman, and who had likewise desired reconciliation. Of course he was acquitted.

"The jury had much difficulty in making up their verdict. Some of them being men of considerable reputation, hesitated long. They could not acquit; they *would* not convict;—and hence a course was taken which corresponded neither with the law nor the evidence.—A verdict of *"justifiable homicide"* was returned, in consequence of which Capt. Gillespie was discharged on his recognizance to appear in the court of King's Bench the ensuing term, and plead his Majesty's pardon."

Such is the account which Sir Jonah gives of his unfortunate brother William's death. It bears heavy on the fame of General Gillespie, and before we gave it to the public, his family had an opportunity to correct it.

After having given so many instances of danger in the arduous office of a Second, we hope that husbands and fathers may in future stand excused from that responsible situation in a duel, which can only with propriety be filled by such gentlemen as O'Gorman Mahon, who with great personal courage unites humanity and common sense. "Filling," says this estimable Irishman, "the situations we do (at all times infinitely more responsible and irksome than that of *principals*) we should not be too fastidious in making mutual concessions to ensure so laudable an end as that of reconciliation. It is true, we may subject ourselves to charges of being over liberal in our anxiety to adjust this without hostile collision, but such observations generally emanate from those who have themselves least taste for fighting."

What Ganganelli said to the confessor of a convent is equally applicable to the second in a duel, "There are occasions on which it will be necessary to exercise all your firmness, and without which you cannot be the director but the directed. If you neglect these hints you will repent it."

SUCCESSFUL INTERFERENCE

"Who saves a life, deserves a civic crown."

The country people interfered in a desperate case between Messrs. M——t and M——y, near Sligo, in 1826, insisting that the two shots each, which had been already fired, afforded ample satisfaction for any possible offence, and that they would not suffer "the gintlemin to murdther one another."—The peasantry of Roscommon behaved in a similar manner, when two gentlemen from Longford made an appointment in their neighbourhood. The parties were in this case forcibly disarmed by the peasantry, until they pledged their honor that their difference was at an end.

In 1783, a passing clergyman succeeded in reconciling two gentlemen, who were preparing to fight a duel at Kensington Gravel Pits.—Mr. Christopher Bentham, of Dublin, was also successful, after many ineffectual efforts, in reconciling two gentlemen, who were in the act of fighting a duel near Milltown.— The particulars of this transaction will be found in a future page.

Our late worthy, talented, and much-lamented friend, John Adrien, the surgeon, whose mantle has descended on his son, had much experience on the point of honor, and was frequently appealed to for his opinion on the ground. Having been called upon, in his professional capacity, to attend a Mr. Cassidy, who was aged about nineteen, and a Mr. O'Neil, aged sixty, the surgeon found the parties were proceeding, after two shots each, to fight about a blow, which Lieutenant Everard, one of the seconds, alleged was given by Mr. Cassidy to his friend, Mr. O'Neil, but which neither of the principals remembered any thing about. An apology had been offered by Lieutenant Douglas, on the part of Mr. Cassidy, for this asserted blow, but strange to say, it was objected to by Mr. Everard. Adrien was appealed to—he had a head to judge, a heart to feel, and a persuasive tongue to plead with. Cassidy broke ground—approached his adversary—expressed his sorrow for the cause of their appointment, and was embraced, with tears of joy and of affectation, by a man who might have been his victim at the next discharge.

When it was announced by the papers that Mr. O'Connell had arrived in London, and was on his way to the continent to fight Mr. Peele, information was given to the magistrates, and the parties were arrested.

The Rev. Mr. L'Estrange gave information at a police office, and had warrants issued for the arrest of Messrs. Maurice O'Connell and Darcy Mahon.

Mr. Cole, a police magistrate, having witnessed a transaction in the boxes of the Dublin theatre which was likely to produce a duel, bound the parties to preserve the peace. His conduct was afterwards approved of by the Judges in the court of King's Bench.

The Speakers of the Lords and Commons, both in Westminster and Dublin, have frequently interposed successfully.

Mr. Curran once effected a reconciliation by a joke, which put the Irish House of Commons in great good humour. The following particulars of this transaction have been placed on record by one of the principals. After many years of great familiarity and friendship, some warmth occurred between Messrs. Toler and Barrington. On the return of the former from Lord Clare's, where he had dined, Barrington said, the other had a hand for every man, and a heart for nobody. A warm answer was given, and a wink invited Barrington to follow, which he did without delay; but the Speaker sent the serjeant at arms to arrest them both. Toler was caught by the skirts of his coat, which were completely torn off. Barrington was laid hold of in Nassau-street, and carried, like a sack, on a man's shoulders to the Commons, amidst the shoutings of the mob. Toler got up to justify his conduct, but having no skirt, appeared so ridiculous, that the ever-ready Curran turned the whole into good humour, by saying, it was an unparalleled insult to the house for one member to *trim* the *jacket* of another within the walls, and nearly within view of the Speaker.

Lord Coleraine, formerly known by the familiar appellation of *Blue Hanger,* from the colour of his clothes, was, perhaps, the best dressed man of his age; and he was no less remarkable for his politeness and good humour. Heavy losses at play, when he was a young man, compelled him to retire to France; and there he remained upwards of twelve years, until the death of his elder brother, when he came to the title, and returned to this country, a complete Frenchman.

On his lordship's first visit to Drury-lane theatre, his natural turn for pleasantry brought him into a *rencontre* that gave him some uneasiness. Seeing a gentleman in *boots* enter the box where he was sitting (in the dress circle,) and place himself on the seat before him rather abruptly, his ideas of etiquette could not well brook what in France would be considered as a breach of decorum; accordingly he addressed him in the following words. "I beg, Sir, you will make no apology." "Apology, for what?" "Why," returned his Lordship pointing down towards the boots, "that you did not bring your horse with you into the box." "Perhaps it is lucky for you, Sir," retorted the stranger, "that I did not bring my *horsewhip;* but I have a remedy at hand, for I can pull your nose for your impertinence." Some other gentlemen in the box now interfered, an exchange of cards took place, and both parties left the theatre.

Blue went immediately to his brother George at Brookes's, and having stated the particulars, begged his assistance to get out of the scrape, "which," said he, "may end in bloodshed.—I acknowledge," he continued, "that I was the first aggressor; but it was too bad to threaten to pull my nose. What had I better do?" *"Soap it well,"* replied George, "and then it will easily slip through the fingers." George, however, accommodated the affair to the satisfaction of all parties, by explaining to the stranger, that his brother had resided so long in France as almost to forget the customs of his countrymen.

This method of avoiding a hearty tweak of the proboscis, appears to have been a favourite of Colonel Hanger's, for he recommends it even in the Memoirs of his life;—he says, that whenever any person is inclined to calumniate a gentleman behind his back, he ought to take the precaution of *soaping his nose first.*

We have an account in the History of London, of a meeting,

at early dawn, of thirty gentlemen on each side, in Moorfields, then a sequestered spot, to decide a private quarrel. The place was in front of the madhouse, and the preparations for the combat excited the lively attention of the inhabitants. As soon as the combatants, drawn up in opposite ranks, set to, the madmen, seized with an uncontrollable fury, broke out of their wooden house, armed with bludgeons and such weapons as they could collect, they assailed the combatants, whose arms availed nothing when opposed to the rage of madness, and they were all soon dispersed, after receiving a sound drubbing.

Before he left Castlebar, Judge Burton having learned that an affair of honor was in contemplation, had the parties, Lord Bingham and Mr. James Browne, brought before him, and bound them and sureties in recognizance to keep the peace, to the amount of nine or ten thousand pounds on each side. His Lordship warned them, that if they went to France and had meeting there, they and their bail would forfeit their recognizance. This is a point of law too little known.

In March 1750 Admiral Knowles and Capt. H——s fought with pistols; several shots were fired without effect; and his Majesty hearing that four other officers had challenged the admiral, had them all put under arrest.—His late Majesty having a particular esteem for the unfortunate Harvey Aston, and knowing his propensity to duelling which his Majesty deplored, exacted a promise from that gentleman, that he would not fight again, a promise in the violation of which he died. It was said, that this benevolent sovereign once required a pledge from a certain Irish secretary, that he would not notice any thing offensive to his feelings, in the discharge of what he undertook as a public duty.

Mr. Hanway says, "the greatest misfortune attending the prelude to a duel, is the frequent carelessness or too great confidence in a supposed accommodation, on the parts of the bye-standers, or of the friends of the parties contending; to which we may add, the supposed shame of the parties themselves, in asking advice in such cases. I have been more than once assured by a very gallant sea-officer, who has given proof of his courage upon the most important occasions, that he had been instrumental in making up near a dozen quarrels, which to all appearance must have proceeded to the extremity of a duel."

Before we close this article upon conciliatory interference, we would remind all seconds and advisers, that in cases where they conceive it is necessary to make an apology or to stand a shot, without returning the fire, the former is to be preferred as the more honorable; because after a man sustains an injury for which he is entitled to redress, it is unjust to expose him, and such of his friends as have reason to expect a duel, to the uncomfortable feelings of which the strongest minds cannot but be susceptible, until the result of the quarrel shall be known.

Conciliation never can be attempted too soon; and until the combat shall have ceased, it should never be abandoned by the friends or other persons on the ground:—who may say with Shakespeare,

> "The nobler action is
> In virtue than in vengeance."

or with Homer:—"Subdue thy mighty rage; it is by no means necessary for thee to have a merciless heart. Even the Gods themselves are flexible. Even these, when any one may transgress or err, do men divert from anger, by sacrifices and appeasing vows."

As gentlemen acknowledge their equality by the sending or accepting of a challenge, there should be no imperfect reconciliations; each should say, with the great Bard of Avon,

> "He being here,
> The sole drift of our purpose, wrath now ends;
> Not a frown further."

Justified by our own experience during many years, and that of several friends, as well as by the thousands of anecdotes and cases which we have collected, we now fearlessly assert, that unless where there is at least one ruffian, there are very few cases in which an honorable reconciliation cannot be easily effected, without a reference to the *dernier resort*.

IMPRUDENCE OF FRIENDS
AND RELATIVES

"Oh! that my friend should be my murderer."

In the case of Colclough and Alcock, we have the opinion of Baron Smith, "that there was room for more conciliation than was tried; and that the deceased (Mr. Colclough) fell a victim to the intemperance of his own friends. This, indeed, (continued the learned judge,) is a melancholy truth, from which no person who has heard this trial can withhold his sad assent. No person, who believes the evidence, can entertain a doubt, that though the deceased perished by the shot of a pistol which was held by Mr. Alcock, yet there is a sense in which it may be questioned whether this implement of death was delivered to him by Mr. King, (one of the seconds,) or forced into his hand by a friend of Mr. Colclough's. The next witness, gentlemen, was the Rev. Mr. Colclough, whom we find pursuing a line of conduct which it were to be wished that others had adopted: a conduct at once becoming the sacred character which he filled, and proving him to be what he professed himself,—a friend of the deceased."

In a fatal duel between Major Clarke and Mr. Featherston, the quarrel was about a recruit, to whom each had obstinately preferred a claim, and the father of Mr. F. is said to have laid an injunction on his son, never to return from the ground until he had taken the life of his adversary, with whom we were intimately acquainted, and from whom we had all the particulars of the quarrel.

In Sept. 1824, a duel took place at Dominica, between two coloured lads, Damas and Rainy, neither of whom were sixteen years of age. The former, whose mother was on the ground was killed, and the survivor was encouraged by his father.

The fathers of two boys, aged sixteen, encouraged them in a duel, near Augusta; and one of them was present when his son was killed by a rifle ball.

When Mr. Luke Keefe shot Mr. Fitzgerald, near Athy, the father of the victim was generally blamed for the part he took in the transaction.

Corneille makes such a father say to his son:—

> "Against his arrogance go try thy courage;
> In blood alone such outrages are wash'd;
> Or kill or die."

A female relative of Mr. William Barrington, having indiscreetly spoken of the difference between that gentleman and Lieutenant M'Kenzie, led to two duels, in the last of which her brother fell a victim by the hand of Captain Gillespie.

A duel between Mr. John Davis and Captain Hearn took place near Kilkenny. Captain Hearn was killed by the second shot, and a relation who was interested in his death, was considerably blamed for the promotion of the duel.

Mr. D'Esterre owed his death to the imprudence of his friends, who urged him to take up a quarrel which did not belong to him, and which, in the event of Mr. O'Connell's death, might have led to the most serious consequences.

We trust that friends and relatives will no more be found exciting quarrels, or accompanying parties to the ground, except for purposes of reconciliation.

TRIFLING CAUSES OF QUARREL

"What are you fighting about—you two?
Why, my eyes are grey, and his are blue."

It may amuse our readers to be informed that the above motto has been taken from Poor Humphrey's Almanack, where it is associated with Saturday, the 21st of March, 1829, the very day on which his Grace of Wellington and the Earl of Winchilsea met in mortal combat, which could have been with ease prevented, by referring to a Court of Honor.

"Resentments of this sort," says Jonas Hanway, "ought on all accounts to be referred to a Court of Honor, which may easily accommodate such a quarrel, when men really mean to act like men."

Lieutenant Newman was killed by a brother officer at Athlone. The cause of quarrel was some slight offence received while the parties were playing what is generally termed leap-frog. Newman was shot through the nose, lived a considerable time in the greatest agony, and after literally starving to death, in consequence of the obstruction to his swallowing nourishment, he left a wife and four unprovided children to lament his loss.

The nephew of a French minister was killed very lately at Strasburgh, in a duel, which arose about a question whether a certain ungovernable horse could possibly be trained within three days.

In a duel at Eyrecourt, Mr. Donnellan killed Mr. Callanan, who was his bosom friend and school-fellow. The quarrel was about a neck handkerchief, which the latter lent to the former when absent from home.

Sir George Ramsay's fatal quarrel in 1790, originated in a blow given by Captain Macrae, at the Edinburgh theatre door, to the servant of Sir George, for some alleged misconduct, and the refusal of that gentleman to dismiss him for the offence. Sir George was shot nearly through the heart, and lingered for a few days in great agony. His death had such an effect upon the mind of the unfortunate servant, that he fell into strong convulsions from which he never recovered.

The fatal duel between Messrs. Montgomery and Macnamara, arose from a very trifling blow given by one of those gentlemen to a dog belonging to the other; affording an additional evidence, that the man who is too captious, walks in the shadow of death, and on the verge of his sepulchre.

An Irish officer, at the Army and Navy Coffee-house, St. Martin's-lane, said, he had seen fifty acres of anchovies, which produced an exclamation from the company. Indignant that his veracity should be questioned, he called the man who doubted him a rascal. A meeting was arranged, and just as they were preparing to discharge the second case of pistols, the Irishman ran up to his antagonist, apologizing for his great mistake in using the word *anchovies* instead of *capers.*

In July, 1828, a case was entertained at Bow-street, in which two gentlemen had quarrelled about the use of a coal-hole; in consequence of which, one of them dispatched an invitation to the other, that he would do him the favor to come and be shot at, before the usual hour for breakfast.

Dr. Dodd tells us, that a challenge was sent to a gentleman for abruptly leaving a room in which the challenger had been holding forth upon some subject, less interesting to others than to himself.

Sterne's father fought with Captain Phillips about a goose.— Major D'Arcy brought out Major Dawson for asking him to take "another tumbler" of the oblivious beverage.—But, perhaps, the case of General Barry and a Captain Smith is one of the most extraordinary which has ever yet occurred. The editor of the Morning Chronicle gives the following account of it; but the full particulars we purposely reserve for the collection of Naval and Military Quarrels, in the second volume.

"A case at Bow-street, affords a striking illustration of the difficulty of guarding by any degree of caution against the liability to quarrel. Captain Smith and General Barry were passengers in one of the steam packets from Ireland to this country, and while at dinner, the Captain asked the General to take wine with him, which the other declined, as, when at sea, wine or spirits made him ill. This was construed by the other party into an affront, which required explanation or the alternative of *meeting*.

"So much for the incident, which might, but for the good sense of General Barry, have led to a loss of human life. To an Englishman it is difficult to imagine how any man could conceive such an incident, on the most unfavourable supposition, afforded him the slightest ground for personal quarrel. He might feel mortified, or piqued, but he would never dream that he was called upon to cut down all whose demeanour did not come exactly up to his idea of propriety. He would never think of proceeding to the extremity of taking away the life of another, or risking his own, without a ground of justification, with which he could satisfy his own conscience."

QUARRELS ARISING FROM MISTAKES

"Shame on you both, young gentlemen,
Your quarrel hath no base on which to stand."

Sir Jonah Barrington, when in college, fought a duel with Mr. Richard Daly, afterwards the patentee of the Dublin theatre, upon whose invitation he repaired to Donnybrook, without having had the slightest quarrel, or any acquaintance previously. Barrington was confounded with another gentleman: but the fight could not be spoiled upon such trifling grounds, and both the parties were hit. The case will be found amongst the Quarrels of the Bar, in volume the third, as Mr. Daly was a Templar at the period of the duel.

Lord Kilmaurs, the Earl of Glencairn's eldest son, being at the theatre in Marseilles, spoke rather loudly, being very deaf himself. A French officer, unacquainted with the infirmity of his lordship, and displeased with the noise, repeatedly cried *paix,* or be quiet.—Lord Kilmaurs did not hear this, and continuing to talk loudly, the officer said, with a very fierce look, *Taizez vous,* or "hold your tongue." This led to a fatal duel.

A duel was fought in a field near Highgate, in May 1826, between a Mr. N. T. S——s, a young Irish gentleman, and a Mr. B——ni, an Italian. The former was attended by Captain W., and the latter by Mr. E——ton. Mr. B. fired first, and missed; upon which Mr. S. discharged his pistol in the air, which put an end to the affair. The quarrel originated the evening before, in Portland-place; where Mr. S. horsewhipped Mr. B., having mistaken him for another Italian gentleman, whom he much resembled. Mr. S. on being convinced of his mistake apologised; but Mr. B. considering that he had carried the joke too far, insisted on a meeting.

A Portuguese officer, at Portsmouth, who was ignorant of the English language, had a quarrel about twenty legs of mutton, which he had ordered for a supper, instead of twenty sheep's trotters. The particulars of this misunderstanding may be found in the Dublin Morning Post of Sept. 29, 1828.

A very near relative of the benevolent Jonas Hanway was once attacked in the open street by one of those "fighting gentlemen" who it seems took him for another person. He retired, and said, for heaven's sake forbear; I never saw you before, nor know I who you are: this however did not restrain the aggressor. His eyes were as blind as his heart: he pushed forward, and as the price of his rashness he received a mortal wound, only living long enough to ask pardon for his mistake.

Lieutenant Crowther was the victim of a grievous mistake on the part of Captain Helsham.—The case of Lord Byron and Thomas Moore arose from a misunderstanding;—and the fatal affair between Messrs. Anderson and Stephens, arose out of a supposed offence.

On the 13th of May, 1828, a Mr. H. of Hardwicke-street, stated in the Dublin papers, that he had accepted a written apology for the insult which a distinguished individual had offered him on the 13th of December, *which insult originated in mistake;* and that motives of delicacy induced him not to name the party.

When any quarrel happens to originate in a mistake, even though a blow, or the most injurious language, should have passed between the parties, it is much more reasonable to interchange apologies than shots. The man who thinks himself aggrieved, should experience great indulgence for the excitement under which he may have acted; and the object of his wrath must always stand approved by good men, for lessening the difficulties in the way of an adjustment.

DUELS BETWEEN BROTHERS

"My brother! Oh my brother!"

"Have you not love enough to bear with me,
    When that rash humour which my mother gave me,
Makes me forgetful."

U nder the head of Miscellaneous Quarrels, we shall give an
interesting detail of the fatal duel which was fought upon
the ground still known by the name of the Brothers' Steps.

In March, 1691, Thomas and Edward Cecil, sons to the third
Earl of Salisbury, fought and severely wounded each other at
St. Germain's. After the duel, they were completely reconciled;
asked mutual forgiveness; sent for a Catholic priest, and prepared for another world. The eldest, who was but nineteen, died
of his wounds; the younger, with great difficulty, was restored to
health; and shocked at the memory of his brother's fate, he
threw himself into the cloisters of La Trappe.

Two brothers, distractedly in love with the same woman, met
with pistols in the Bois de Boulogne, and tossed up for the first
fire; the eldest gained it. He took his ground at three paces,
aimed at his brother, and hit him in the left side. No sooner did
the younger see his blood flow, than he darted on his brother,
and shot him dead. Remorse succeeded: he cast himself upon
the body—embraced his victim—and watered him with tears.
He then sought preservation by flying from Paris; but believing
himself to be pursued every where by the ghost of his murdered
brother, he gave himself up to justice at Dijon.

Who will venture to be so base in future, as to be a second, or
bystander, when two brothers fight? We hope the press may
hang him on a literary gibbet for the public good.

DUELS BETWEEN FRIENDS

"What rage, oh friends! what fury
Doth you to these dire actions hurry?
What towns, what garrisons, might you
With hazard of this blood subdue,
Which now y' are bent to throw away
In vain untriumphable fray."

At New York, Mr. Barton shot Mr. Graham with whom he had long been upon terms of great intimacy. Two officers of the name of Nesbitt, who were friends and near relations, fought in Athlone.—And two cousins of the name of Powel, who were members of the Irish Bar, fought a fatal duel in Dublin. John Colclough was killed by his own friend, Alcock,

"But happier in my mind, was he that died,
For many deaths has the survivor suffered!"

Mr. Alcock lost his senses after the duel, and a similar fate attended another survivor of a duel which was fought near Cork.—Two friends quarrelled at a billiard table in the town of Cashel, one was a celebrated shot, and the other inexperienced and pacific; attempts were made to reconcile them, but the brother of the duellist urged him to his own destruction, and insisted on a meeting of the parties, which took place in a churchyard at New Inn. The combatants were placed at opposite angles of the ground, and having received their pistols from the seconds, were allowed to advance and fire at any distance they thought proper. He who was encouraged by his *brother*, being accustomed to hit the ace of spades at forty yards, declared that he would shoot his adversary at that distance; but failing in the attempt to do so, he was himself the victim of a man who had but little practice with a pistol, and who was habitually peaceable.

In 1769, a captain and lieutenant of marines, who were bosom friends, fought at Plymouth, under the influence of liquor.

Messrs. Stuart and Dade were intimate friends, and nearly next door neighbours in King George's County, Virginia. Their quarrel was about a very trifling matter, and they met upon the Maryland shore, in August or September, 1820, opposite their own houses, at a very short distance, having muskets loaded with buck shot, of which Mr. Stuart received so many, that he expired in a few hours.

In July, 1824, a duel was fought in Paris between Lieutenant Finch and a Mr. Beeby, who were formerly most intimate acquaintances, but had grown cool in their friendship in consequence of some trifling misunderstanding, which remained unsettled, until Finch offended a clergyman, whose friends demanded satisfaction. Mr. F. would give none; and it was therefore proposed that he should chuse his antagonist amongst the parson's friends. He chose Mr. Beeby; alledging that the old misunderstanding could be adjusted with that gentleman, while he vindicated the clergyman. They met, and Mr. Beeby fell under the first discharge.

Messrs. Fenshaw and Hartinger having quarrelled about a female relative, met on the race course at Ascot Heath, in September, 1820. They were friends and near relatives. A fruitless attempt was made to reconcile them after the first fire; and in the third, both were very severely wounded.

The inexorable spirit which has been evinced by friends in quarrel, has been thus described by M. Corneille:—

> "'Tis little to neglect so strong a duty,
> That my own heart declares thee innocent:
> 'Tis little which it gives to public error;
> Thou art a criminal since thou art accus'd.
> My wounded honor knows too well its due,
> Not to revenge on thee what men believe.
> Such is the unpitiable law of honor,
> When injured by a friend, to mind itself alone;
> In its own cause, ever inexorable,
> It asks the dearest blood if but thought guilty."

The celebrated Earl of Chesterfield having discovered that two incendiaries were endeavouring to promote a duel between himself and a very particular friend, arranged with him that the incendiaries should be the seconds, and that the quarrel should go on until the principals received the fatal signal, but that instead of firing they should march off together, leaving the seconds on the ground to reflect on their improper conduct: a plan which was admirably carried into execution, for the principals had sufficient influence to provide that, previous to their firing, they should be placed back to back at the usual distance. Instead of turning, upon the signal being given, each marched off in opposite directions, to the unexpected mortification of their treacherous seconds.

Sir Richard Steele, in the Conscious Lovers, puts the following sentiments into the mouth of Myrtle.—"How many friends have died by the hands of friends, for the want of temper."

QUARRELSOME PERSONS

"Bullies are ever cowards, cowards bullies."

The author of a valuable work on war, says, "He that is easily offended will also easily offend. The man who is always on the alert to discover trespasses on his honor or his rights, never fails to quarrel with his neighbours. Such a person may be dreaded as a torpedo, but he will seldom procure respect, and never conciliate regard; and him whom we neither love nor honor, we often are indifferent whether we displease. There are, therefore, many feuds and litigations in the life of such a man, that would never have disturbed its quiet, if he had not captiously snarled at the trespasses of accident, and savagely retaliated insignificant injuries. The viper that we chance to molest, we suffer to live if he continue to be quiet; but if he raises himself in menaces of destruction, we knock him on the head."

When two persons, of a turbulent and quarrelsome disposition, were brought before Philip of Macedon for his judgment, he is reported to have passed on them the following judicious sentence: "You," said he to the one, "I command immediately to run out of Macedon; and you," turning to the other, "see that you make all imaginable haste after him." Thus banishing them from a civilized capital, as common nuisances to society. "A good riddance," says the historian, of such salamanders as delight to live in the fire of contention; commencing sharp quarrels upon trivial accounts, and withal knowing no time wherein to end them."

In a future volume we shall give an interesting picture of that imp and ruffian, George Robert Fitzgerald; who fought thirty duels, and was afterwards hanged for murder. Having teazed Lieutenant Thompson, on his return from a review, and trodden on his toes at a ball the same evening, they proceeded unattended to a garden, and locked the door inside. After an ineffectual effort on the part of Thompson to obtain a competent apology for the offence he had received, he desired Fitzgerald to choose the ground and the distance. "Here I am," said Fitzgerald, "fire away." At the second fire Fitzgerald was struck above the temple, upon which he staggered, groaned, and fell. Some neighbours, hearing the reports of pistols, forced the garden door, and found Thompson prostrate, weeping over the body of his adversary. He accused himself of the murder, and offered himself a willing victim to the laws. On Fitzgerald's removal, it was found that trepanning was necessary; and the patient begged of the surgeons, in the most pathetic manner, that his toupée might not be injured in the operation.

On another occasion, Fitzgerald proceeded, with arms, to the door of the Honorable Collector Browne; abused him grossly as a coward, and insisted upon an immediate meeting, with small swords or pistols.—Browne preferred the broad sword; and was proceeding, with his weapon under his arm, to a friend whom he wished to act as a second, when Fitzgerald suddenly renewed the charge of cowardice, and fired a loaded pistol at Browne, which made the Collector hastily return to his house.

Fitzgerald once followed Richard Martin, the late member for the county of Galway, to the Dublin theatre, struck him with his cane, and said, "take that, you scoundrel." Mr. Martin sent him a message by a Mr. Lyster, who received a caning for his interference. It was long before Martin could obtain redress. A meeting was at length agreed upon, in the barrack yard of Castlebar, at the distance of nine yards. Here the ruffian twice interrupted the aim of Mr. Martin, when he found that point-blank marksman had him covered. He first said, "Martin, I am not prepared;" which induced his adversary to let down his pistol. The second interruption was occasioned by his crying out, "there's blood in your eye, cousin Dick, take down your pistol." At the second discharge of pistols both the principals were wounded.

Cæsar French once ordered Captain Fitzgerald to draw, in Castlebar. After several passes, French was wounded in the hip, and would have slain Fitzgerald, if he had not thrown himself upon the ground, as if by accident; which Mr. French was too high minded to take the least advantage of.

This truly infamous character was introduced to the King of France by the English ambassador, with an assurance that he had fought six and twenty fatal duels. The king contented himself by saying, that Mr. Fitzgerald's life would form an excellent companion for that of Jack the Giant-killer.

Amongst the professed duellists who occupy a place in our portfolio, are Messrs. M'Manus, M'Neil, Hardiman, Scroggs, and Marriott; officers who, upon the conclusion of the treaty at Utrecht, became nuisances to civilized society, into which they intruded for the sole purpose of exciting duels, and were shunned by all the other officers. M'Manus was sent to the West Indies, where he was involved in many quarrels, until a planter, after many unusual provocations, called him out and shot him. M'Neil was hanged. Hardiman, after killing five Irishmen in duels, under circumstances which were not considered very honorable, died in bed, to the astonishment of those who knew him.—Scroggs and Marriott having quarrelled, fell, fortunately for society, by each other's swords.

The following is one of the many instances which might be quoted, to shew that duelling is not always an evidence of real courage. During the German war, an officer serving under the Duke of Cumberland, was observed to evince very great cowardice in every engagement; yet he was remarkable for a quarrelsome disposition, and scarcely a week elapsed in which he did not fight a duel: this occasioned his Royal Highness to exclaim, "It is an extraordinary circumstance that I have under my command one of the rankest cowards, and yet there is not a man who dares to tell him so."

We shall reserve some remarks and anecdotes upon this subject, until we come to speak of courage.

TRICKS AND STRATAGEMS

"He being remiss,
Most generous, and free from all contriving,
Will not peruse the foils; so that with ease,
Or with a little shuffling, you may choose
A sword unbated. I'll have prefer'd him
A chalice for the nonce; whereon but sipping,
If he by chance escape your venomed stuck,
Our purpose may hold there."

The honor of some adversaries can never be relied on safely. In a selfish or revengeful spirit, many persons might be disposed to commit assassination, for which reason, friends and time are always indispensible.

In the case of Xanthus and Melancthus, which Strabo has related, it was agreed that the combatants should come into the field without any attendants, but however as they were preparing to encounter, Melancthus cried out that the conditions had been broken, for that Xanthus had somebody with him, upon which the latter incautiously looking round him, was treacherously slain by his antagonist.

In the case of Pittacus and Phryno, the former carried a net very secretly with his buckler, which having thrown over his unsuspecting adversary, he easily overcame and slew him.

A treacherous duel was fought at Ostuni, in 1664, between the Count of Conversano and the Duke of Martino. After a war of words, the Count challenged the Prince of Francavilla to decide their difference by the sword: the latter, being aged and infirm, gave the preference to pistols; the Count, who was one of the best swordsmen in the kingdom, persisted in his first proposal, and in order to provoke the Prince struck him repeatedly with the flat side of his sheathed sword. This assault being public, the viceroy ordered the aggressor's immediate arrest, and subsequently that both parties should retire to their respective estates. The prince, however, proposed his nephew, the Duke of Martino, as his champion, and a year was allowed for preparation; during which time, a gentleman who was a retainer in the prince's family, left it abruptly one night for Conversano's castle, where, by the recital of fictitious wrongs endured from the Prince of Francavilla, he obtained a favorable reception; and being an excellent swordsman, the count continually practised fencing with him. When the renegado had acquired a sufficient knowledge of the count's particular mode of fighting, he returned to the prince, upon the pretext of a visit to relations, and acquainted the Duke of Martino, that his only chance of success depended upon his keeping on his defence in the earlier stages of the combat; that the count being corpulent and violent, would be speedily exhausted by his own impetuosity. They met; the count was slain by a second wound, after refusing to be reconciled upon receiving the first; and the prince had prepared a band of assassins, who would have murdered him on his return from the field, in the event of his being the victor.

Under the head of Quarrelsome Persons, will be found some anecdotes of treachery, by that accomplished ruffian George Robert Fitzgerald.

The Sieur Chelais, a member of the French Parliament, was condemned to be broken on the wheel in 1769, for the murder of Sieur Beguin, a captain in the Legion of Flanders, whom he challenged and killed. It appeared that Chelais had put on private armour.—When his adversary's sword was broken against the armour, he fell, and was stabbed on the ground by Chelais.

At a special term of the circuit court for St. Clair County at Bellville, Timothy Bennett was tried for the murder of Alphonso C. Stewart, committed in February 1819. It appeared that the dispute between Bennett and Stewart arose from the loss of a mare belonging to Bennett, which he supposed had been killed by Stewart. The parties met at a tavern at Belleville, when it was proposed that Stewart should challenge Bennett, the proposers assuring Stewart that it should be a *sham duel*. The challenge was accordingly sent, and accepted by Bennett. The seconds loaded the rifles with powder only, taking care to slip the balls, which were in their hands, into their sleeves. Bennett was seen to put a ball into his rifle, after his second had handed it to him. They then went into the public street, took their distance, and fired. Stewart was shot through the heart and fell.—Bennett was immediately arrested, examined, and sent to prison, whence he escaped the evening previous to the day appointed for his trial. He was apprehended near St. Genevieve, and again confined in the Belleville Gaol. The jury, after a patient investigation of the case, returned a verdict of guilty, and he was sentenced to be hung.

Thomas Ramsay and Joseph Higginbotham fought a duel in a room at Dunlavin. Having but one pistol, they tossed for the first shot, which was won by Ramsay. After charging it with powder only, he, with apparent generosity, gave up the shot to his antagonist, who unfortunately accepted of the treacherous present, and used it without doing any injury to Ramsay; who next proceeded to load with a ball for his own use; this was objected to by a Mr. Handwich, who knew how the pistol had been prepared before; he, however, was immediately turned out of the room by Ramsay and a person named Freeman. Mr. Higginbotham was severely wounded, and did not recover for about two years, a portion of his waistcoat having been carried by the ball into his lungs. He was afterwards murdered by one Duffy, at a place called Narrowmore.—Ramsay and Freeman fled after the duel; the former turned robber, and was hung at Wexford for the robbery of Mr. Masterson.

On the borders of Austria and Turkey, where a private quarrel might occasion the massacre of a whole family or village, the desolation of a province, and, perhaps, even the more extended horrors of a national war; when any serious dispute arises between the subjects of the different empires, recourse is had to what is called *the custom of the frontier.* A spacious plain or field is selected, whither, on an appointed day, judges of the respective nations repair, accompanied by all those whom curiosity or interest may attract together. The combatants are not restricted in the choice or number of their arms, or in their method of fighting, but each is at liberty to employ whatever he conceives is most advantageous to himself, and to avail himself, also, of any artifice which may ensure his own safety, or destroy the life of his antagonist. The circumstances of one frontier combat were particularly extraordinary: the German, armed with the barrel of a rifle pistol, mounted on a carabine stock, placed himself in the middle of the field; and conscious that he could at once destroy the Turk, who was his adversary, when he came within a certain distance, began to smoke his pipe with great composure. The Turk, with two pistols in his belt, two in his breast, two others in his holsters, and a dagger and a sabre at his side, advanced like a moving magazine, and galloping round the German kept continually firing at him. The German, conscious that little was to be apprehended from such a marksman and such weapons, continued still to smoke his pipe; the Turk, at length, observing a little explosion, as if his adversary's pistol had missed fire, advanced with great rapidity to cut him down, and was almost instantly shot dead. The wily German had put some gunpowder into his pipe, and the flash, as he expected, had deceived the Turk.

A Frenchman and a Hanoverian, who were both officers of cavalry, had a quarrel at Corfu: the latter of gigantic stature, and the former very small. They fought with sabres for a full half hour, during which time the Hanoverian having made several efforts to cut down his adversary, was thrown into a great passion and a profuse perspiration. He renewed his efforts to cut down the Frenchman, who threw himself towards the Hanoverian in a sort of inclined plane, and while the sabre fell with trifling force along his back he disengaged the bowels of his powerful assailant who expired in a few minutes. The seconds cried out slaughter, and made a fair report to General Donzelot who pardoned the survivor, alledging that two such officers could not then be spared.

We have heard of a duel between a Frenchman and a Neapolitan. One was a fencing master and the other was his pupil; the latter by ingeniously casting his slipper backwards in the air, distracted the attention of his more skilful master, and slew him when he found him off his guard.

Mr. Thomas Fenton, when acting as the second of his relative, John Fenton, was accused of having unfairly stood too long conversing with his principal; because, while standing between the parties, he enabled John Fenton to look over his shoulder, and take deliberate aim at Major Ellis, who fell at the first shot.

In the case of Messrs. Kyan and Dillon, at Galway, in 1816,

the word was given by Mr. Kyan's second, and the friend of Mr. Dillon screened him, until he covered his adversary, who could not have an equal view. Mr. Kyan was shot dead, while in the very act of taking the pistol off his left arm, on which it had been balanced, for the purpose of wiping his eyes, and taking a pinch of snuff. He was an excellent shot, an experienced duellist, the first person who had put a duelling pistol into Dillon's hand, and who had frequently been his second in the field.

Governor Wall killed a gentleman in India, under such foul circumstances, that his brother officers refused to associate with him, and he was obliged to return to England.

When the Duke of Hamilton fought and killed Lord Mohun, he was stabbed while he lay wounded and helpless on the ground, by Macartney, who had been second to his adversary, as must be evident upon perusal of James Hamilton's trial for aiding and assisting as the second of the Duke.

While Mr. Reynolds was in the act of saluting Mr. Keon, with his hat in his hand, and politely wishing him good morning, the latter shot him through the head. Mr. Plunket, who was second to the murdered gentleman, exclaimed "shocking!" and Mr. Keon's brother said, "if you do not like it, take that;" snapping a second pistol at Mr. Plunket. For this gross outrage on the laws of honor and of his country, Mr. Keon, the principal, was tried and executed in the Irish capital.

About two months after Mr. Thornhill had been acquitted for shooting Sir Cholmondely Deering in a duel, he was murdered on Turnham Green by two men, who bade him recollect Sir Cholmondely.

RESPONSIBILITY OF THE PRESS

"Put up your sword; for as it is the worst argument, so let it be the last."

In the October of 1825, an attempt was made to hold the editor of the Courant personally responsible for his critiques upon the drama, by Mr. Pritchard, who conceived himself aggrieved on that occasion. The following particulars are copied from the Edinburgh Observer:—

"On Sunday, while the gentleman who is the ostensible editor of the Courant, was attending a funeral in Greyfriars' church-yard, a person, said to be Mr. Pritchard, of the theatre royal, abruptly addressed him to this effect:—'That notwithstanding the solemnity of the occasion, the holy day, and the sacredness of the spot, he could not omit the opportunity of saying, that he would not permit his feelings to be irritated any longer, and that he (meaning the editor of the Courant), was, in his opinion, a scurrilous rascal!' A card was then thrust into the editor's hand, who merely observed, "that this was neither the time nor the place for such conduct and observations;" he immediately tore the card without looking at it, and walked slowly from the church-yard, with the gentlemen who accompanied him. The Courant of yesterday, from which we have taken this account, adds—

"Ignorant as we are of the motives which have tempted the person we have named to so daring a violation of the sanctity of the day and place, and totally unconscious of ever having alluded to him but as an actor, we might leave these facts without comment; but in our private capacity, we feel bound to say, after consulting a friend, by rank and experience in every respect qualified to direct us by his opinion, that the committer of an outrage of a kind so unprecedented—so appalling to all feelings of religion and common decency—is not entitled to other notice than pity. In the exercise of our public duty we have had occasion to criticise the performers of our theatre, and are content to know, that in the general expression of our opinions, we have merely echoed the public voice. We shall not consequently be deterred by conduct, however gross and disgusting, from doing so. We owe the public a duty paramount to every other consideration, and that duty we shall perform, as we have hitherto endeavoured to do, fearlessly and honestly."

Although the case of Colonel Ross and Captain Fottrell might properly be classed with Naval and Military Duels, in another volume, its association with the press decides us upon giving it insertion here; and although we were possessed of a statement which was much more complimentary to Captain Fottrell, we have preferred a very unassuming one, for which we are indebted to his pen.

In December, 1817, a court-martial was held in the Royal Barracks, Dublin, on Quarter Master Jolly, of the fourth dragoon guards, on the charge of having made excessive and exorbitant over-charges on the regimental necessaries furnished to the men of Captain White's troop. A gentleman of the name of Faulkner, who had belonged to the regiment at the time that the circumstances occurred, was called on to give evidence, which he did, in a manner that did him much credit. On the following morning, Mr. F. appeared before the court, and addressed the president, Lord Forbes. After apologizing for his obtrusion, he stated that he had been ten years in that regiment, in the greatest happiness and friendship with all the officers, for whom he still entertained the greatest respect and regard; that he came from a distant part of the country, with great inconvenience to himself, to attend that honorable court; that on his arrival in the barrack-square, he was accosted by an officer, high in regimental rank, who asked him, "had he come to act with the *tailors*, that if he was, he would *cut* him." That after he had given his evidence yesterday, he found that *that* officer had *cut* him. That he did not know how the appellation of *tailor* could apply to him, unless by measuring with his horse-whip the impertinent fellow's jacket:" or words to that effect; at the same time drawing his whip from under his arm.

"This singular address was written out by a friend of mine, who was present, and requested me to get it inserted in one of the public papers, *as an extraordinary military occurrence;* which I did; believing it all to be strictly true; and left word with the editor of the paper, that if any enquiry should be made for the author, my name should at once be given up. On the following day the paragraph appeared, and soon after, Colonel Ross, accompanied by other officers of the same regiment, called at the office of the paper, and enquired who was the author of the paragraph. The proprietor replied, that he was not in the habit of giving up the author of any paragraph which appeared in his paper, unless the truth of it was questioned. They did not then deny the truth of it, and retired. On the following day they again called, and said, that the paragraph *was not strictly true;* whereupon the proprietor declared, as he was authorized to do, that Captain Fottrell, of the Royal Marines, was the author; and that he had Captain Fottrell's instructions to avow it. The proprietor did not know my address. I, therefore, having heard what had passed, went the following morning, (1st January, 1818,) to the Royal Barracks, and was immediately accosted by Captain Hamilton, who asked me if I knew a Captain Fottrell of the Royal Marines. I replied, that I was that person. He then drew from his pocket the paragraph in question, and asked me if I knew any thing of it. I answered that *I was the author*, and that I believed it to be strictly true. He then said, that he was requested by Lieut. Col. Ross to deliver me a message. I replied, that I would give him any satisfaction he required, and that I would immediately go and look for a friend.

"That evening, being disappointed in meeting the friend whom I wished, he being out of town, I waited on Captain Hamilton, and told him of my disappointment; and that, rather than there should be any unnecessary delay, I would go out the following morning unattended, and be perfectly satisfied with any arrangements made by him. He replied, that there was no hurry: in a few days, when my friend came to town, would do.

"To my great surprise, at *ten o'clock that night*, I was waited upon by an orderly dragoon, with a letter from Captain Hamilton, stating, that unless I gave a meeting to Colonel Ross, before two o'clock the following day, an *antidote* to the poison of my paragraph would publicly appear. I replied by letter, that

I did not dread the effects of any antidote which might be attempted, but that I had the good fortune, since I had seen him, to meet a friend who would wait upon him about ten o'clock the following morning. My friend accordingly called upon him, at his rooms in the barracks, and observed, that it was not usual to deliver a message, without first demanding an explanation. Captain Hamilton replied, that they wanted no explanation but *that:*—pointing to a case of pistols which lay on the table. My friend observed, that I was prepared, and would be on the ground (which he named) precisely at two o'clock.

"The parties arrived at the appointed place at the same moment. The friends tossed for the choice of ground, &c. which fell to the lot of Colonel Ross, and was immediately measured—ten paces. It was agreed that we should fire on the words *one, two, three,* being uttered. After the second exchange of shots, I was asked to make an apology. I replied, that having given no offence to Colonel Ross, I would make no apology. On the third exchange, I was asked if I would say, that Colonel Ross was not the officer high in regimental rank alluded to. I replied, that I would not; because I did know, *by report,* that he was the officer alluded to.

"After the fourth exchange, and the fifth pistols being in our hands, and the ground taken, a pause took place, and the following DECLARATION was brought to me:—

'Colonel Ross, I have been brought here to give you satisfaction for the paragraph published by me in Carrick's Morning Post: we have fired four shots each: I now declare, that I did not know, *save from report,* to whom the article alluded which has given you offence; and that I did not otherwise know you to be the officer of high rank mentioned in that article; and being now told, by your friend Captain Hamilton, that the paragraph is incorrect in other particulars, I regret having done so.'

"To this I replied, that I could have no objection to subscribe to that, after the first fire—that, therefore, I had no objection then. Which being done, we approached each other half way, and withdrew from the ground.

"Three shots of mine went through Colonel Ross's clothes: I was not touched. I never exchanged a word with Colonel Ross

until after our first fire; I therefore had no enmity towards him.
I have frequently thanked God for having prevented me from
doing him an injury—my only object was to protect my friend.

"J. FOTTRELL."

Mr. Carrick, who was proprietor of the Dublin Morning Post
at the time when the above circumstances occurred, was a most
respectable gentleman, who would scruple the invasion of
either character or feeling. Colonel Ross, should, in the first
instance, have pointed out what was erroneous; and Mr. Carrick
or Captain Fottrell, after making some enquiry, might have
found themselves justified in making the *amende,* without the
desperate alternative which Captain Hamilton insisted on, when
he laid his hand upon the pistols, and refused all explanation.
We consider it to have been a most unjustifiable and wanton
duel. If any officer in high command should attempt to intimi-
date a witness who was about to discharge a public duty, he
should not feel himself unjustly treated by a statement of the
fact in any honest journal; and before he could have justified a
call upon the writer of the article, he should have pointed out
the words which were at variance with the truth.

Captain Fottrell's generosity and chivalry were far superior to
his prudence. He generously concealed the name of his infor-
mant, because another member of the mess was likely to be *cut;*
and he chivalrously stood four shots, not one of which should
ever have been fired until Colonel Ross disclaimed the imputa-
tion on his honor, and failed in the attainment of full reparation
through the columns of the Post. We wish that we could, even
at this distant period, remove the public impression as to the
origin of this affair; and that we could influence a general determination to accept no challenge for the publication of a fact.

The Age newspaper, at the close of June, 1829, contained the
following passage; of which every gentleman, who is connected
with the press, must candidly admit the truth:—

"Every pest to society, whose black deeds have made him
the terrible but just subject of frequent comment—from the
swindler Semple to the pickpocket Soames, and lastly, the murderer Thurtell—have all of them complained of the prejudice
excited against them by the public press; and would, no doubt,

each and all of them, have applied for criminal informations against the editors, who had done society the service of exposure, if conviction, transportation, or execution, had not happily interfered to prevent their honest intentions."

That our zeal for the independence of the press is not a novelty, may appear by the following quotation from our "School for Patriots and Benevolists," which was published in 1824.

"The patriot will stand, as a sleepless centinel, beside the public press, to see that its rights be not invaded, and he will be compassionate for those peccadilloes, which are always inseparable from human agency, and from momentary excitation.

"Until this invaluable exotic shall be effectually established in our soil, we must be cautious in our prunings, lest we should hazard the existence of the plant; and when, like the venerable cedar on Mount Libanus, it shall be incorporated with the bowels of the land, the screamings of an owl among its branches, cannot scare away the traveller who shall rest beneath its shade.

"'No man,' says Curran, 'is laughed at for a considerable time; every day will furnish some new ridicule to supersede him.' Again he says, 'Every character has a natural station, from which it cannot be effectually degraded, and beyond which it cannot be raised by the brawling of a newspaper: if it is wantonly aspersed, it is but for a season, and that a short one; when it emerges, like the moon from a passing cloud, to its original effulgence.'

"This peerless luminary in the forensic constellation, and inflexible adherent to the public principles which he had adopted, with whose acquaintance we were honored, and whose monument no Vandal can destroy, has sketched the editorial duty with the pencil of a master; and if the public taste be so corrupt as to require a censurable verbiage, let us look to the moral culture of that interesting generation which is to supersede our own, when our playfulness, asperity, and resentment, shall pass the boundary of a country, from whose bourne no traveller can return, until the all-restoring Spirit shall put the dry bones of the valley into motion.

"The press (says Mr. Curran) is the great public monitor; its duty is that of the historian and the witness, that '*Nil falsi audeat, nil veri non audeat dicere,*' that its horizon shall be extended to the farthest verge of truth; that beyond that limit it shall not dare to pass; that it shall speak truth to the king, in the hearing of the people, and to the people in the hearing of the king; that it shall not perplex the one, nor the other, with a false alarm, lest it lose its character for veracity, and become an unheeded warner of a real danger; lest it vainly warn them against that great transgression, of which the inevitable consequence is death.

"For our own part, although we should become the victim of an editorial shaft, or be set aside like Hercules amongst the wrestlers of our nation, yet, while we have a pen to write, or a solitary voice to raise, we shall defend this great public engine with uncompromising faithfulness; because we consider it is convertible into a key-stone for the grand triumphal arch of civil and religious freedom."

Mr. Grattan and Major Edgeworth.

In September, 1827, a severe paragraph appeared in the Freeman's Journal, upon the paving establishment of Dublin, which article gave great offence to a respectable individual, who was one of the Commissioners, and he felt that he had a claim on Mr. Henry Grattan, who was a member of parliament for the city, and the registered proprietor of the offending journal.

In justice to the editor of the Freeman (for the proprietor had no knowledge whatever of the article until it publicly appeared in print), we should remark, that Major Edgeworth's name was never mentioned in it; and that all the observations it contained were of a general description.

In the then distracted state of Ireland, strangers might suppose that politics were secretly mixed up in this transaction; but that such was not the case may easily be ascertained by looking at the Report of the Commissioners appointed to inquire into the management of the Dublin Paving Board, and to the highest ascendency papers of that period.

The Evening Mail, amongst several other remarks upon this board, observed, "that it was profligate, corrupt, and venal:— that its members plundered the public and aggrandized themselves, are facts not to be questioned or denied."

It will appear, by the following documents, that Mr. Grattan was, in the first instance, undecided in the line of conduct which he should pursue; and probably the manner of the delivery had some influence on his declining to accept the challenge. As it was a case which drew forth much of editorial comment—and as Mr. Grattan's having sinned against the press when making the *amende* to the libelled University of Dublin, was not very likely to obtain a prejudiced opinion in his favor, we shall, after publishing the case, make some extracts from his contemporaries, which may be referred to with advantage at a future period.

TO THE EDITOR OF SAUNDER'S NEWS LETTER.

"No. 3, Harcourt Place, Saturday Evening,
"September 15, 1827.

"SIR,—If I am forced into notoriety, the act is certainly not of my own seeking, my character having been falsely and slanderously attacked by a member of the Dublin press in his own paper, and the circumstances which have subsequently occurred in the progress of my attempts to vindicate my honor, being of so peculiar and unprecedented a nature, leave me, unfortunately, no choice but that of submitting the following documents to the public.

"I have the honor to be,
"Your obedient servant,
"T. N. EDGEWORTH."

"36, Harcourt-street, Saturday Evening,
"September 15, 1827.

"MY DEAR EDGEWORTH,—I lost not a moment after you put the *Freeman's Journal* of yesterday, containing the attack upon you, into my hand, when I consented to act as your friend, in proceeding to the Stamp-Office, to ascertain positively, before I waited upon Mr. Henry Grattan, whether he was actually the proprietor of that paper or not. Having satisfied myself that he was the sworn proprietor, I instantly proceeded to his residence in Stephen's-green, determined either to procure the insertion of a contradiction of the offensive paragraph in his paper, which contradiction I had previously prepared, or of demanding the satisfaction due from one gentleman to another, under the circumstances in which you and he were respectively placed.

"On my arrival at his residence, I learned that he was at Tinnehinch, in the County of Wicklow, whither I immediately followed him, having previously left a card with my address, at his house. Unfortunately, however, I was informed at Tinnehinch that he had suddenly left it a short time previous to my arrival, and had returned to Dublin. I did not reach the city until six o'clock in the evening, when I drove directly to Mr. Grattan's house, when I was again informed that he was not at home—I left another card and told the servant that I would call again in half an hour.—At the expiration of that period I did call, and was told that Mr. Grattan was at dinner.—'That,' I said, 'made no difference, as I came on most important business, and must see him.' Mr. Grattan then came out of the dining-room, and showed me into his study. The following is the substance of what occurred, which I transcribe from a note which I committed to paper directly after I left him.

"I commenced by apologising to Mr. Grattan for disturbing him at dinner, and forthwith proceeded to the object of my visit. "I come Sir," said I, "on behalf of my friend, Major Edgeworth, in consequence of a most calumnious attack upon him, contained in your paper of this day." Mr. Grattan started with amazement, and said, "what paper?—my paper!—I know nothing about papers." "Yes, Sir," I replied, "you are the sworn proprietor of *The Freeman's Journal.*" "Well, Sir," said Mr. Grattan, "if you have anything to complain of, you had better go to the people of the office." Annoyed at his attempt to deny his connection with the paper, and nettled at his efforts to shift the thing from himself, I said, with some warmth, "do you suppose, Sir, that Major Edgeworth or I will go looking after your printers or your editor when we have you? He holds you, Sir, responsible for what appears in that paper, and I will make you responsible for it." "I am perfectly acquainted with the *law,*" said Mr. Grattan. "And so am I, Sir," I responded; "but it is the law of *honor*—it is upon that I stand." "Then," said Mr. Grattan, "I suppose the better way will be for me to refer you to a friend." I answered, "decidedly." He then mentioned a Major somebody, but from his hurried manner I was not able distinctly to catch the name, and therefore requested of him to write that with the address, which he was about to do, when, suddenly recollecting himself, he exclaimed, "no; on second thoughts, I will refer you to my friend Mr. Wallace, who on the present occasion, I will call Counsellor Wallace." I asked where I was to wait on him. Mr. Grattan replied, "that he lived in the country, but that he would confer with him immediately."

Upon which I took my leave, saying, "that I should be happy to confer with Mr. Wallace as soon as that communication took place."

Apprehensive lest any misunderstanding might exist, I wrote Mr. Grattan the following note:—No. 1.

> "Friday night, half past nine,
> "36, Harcourt-street.

"Mr. Montgomery presents his compliments to Mr. Henry Grattan, requests to know at what hour in the morning he is to wait on Mr. Grattan's friend, Mr. Wallace.

"Mr. Montgomery would not trouble Mr. Grattan at this period of the evening, but that several hours have been already lost by Mr. Montgomery's not having the good fortune of meeting Mr. Grattan at Tinnehinch this day, whither he followed him from town, not having found him at his residence when he called."

The occurrences which subsequently took place, will be best explained by notes marked Nos. 2, & 3—copies of which I enclose you.

Copy, No. 2.]   "$\frac{1}{4}$-past 12, Saturday.
> "36, Harcourt-street,

"Sir,

"I remained at home until twelve o'clock, expecting either a reply to my note of last night, or a communication announcing that your friend Mr. Wallace had arrived in town.

"At that hour I called at his house in town but did not find him at home.

"I shall be here until two o'clock, by which time I expect to receive a specific reference to Mr. Wallace, or some other friend on your behalf,

> "I have the honor to be,
> "Your obedient servant,
> "JAMES MONTGOMERY."

No. 3.]   "Three o'clock Saturday.
> "36, Harcourt-street.

"Sir,

"Having waited at home half an hour after the time stated in my last note, without receiving any communication from you in reply, either to that or my former application, and having again called upon Mr. Wallace without effect, I beg to state that my friend Major Edgeworth, concluding that you do not mean to give him the satisfaction due to a gentleman, is driven to the only alternative now left him.

> "I have the honor to be,
> "Your obedient servant,
> "JAMES MONTGOMERY."

On my return home at six o'clock this evening, I found a note from Mr. Wallace, of which the following is a copy:—

> "Mr. Wallace's compliments—is sorry he was not at home when Mr. Montgomery called on him to day—he will be at home for about an hour, if Mr. M. has any wish to see him.
> "Saturday evening a quarter past four.
> "—— Montgomery Esq. 36, Harcourt street."

Strictly speaking, I was not bound, after what had occurred, to take any notice of Mr. Grattan, or give him an opportunity of getting out of the very awkward dilemma in which he was placed; but anxious that you should owe nothing to etiquette, or diplomacy; and desirous that the affair between you and him should be adjusted either by a retraction or a meeting, I lost not a moment in waiting on Mr. Wallace. He was again from home when I called, but being expected before his departure for the country, I remained until his return. A very brief statement of what took place will be sufficient for the purpose, which induces this letter.

> "Mr. Wallace said he was not authorised by Mr. Grattan to receive a hostile message from me, and that he (Mr. Grattan) did not consider himself personally responsible to Major Edgeworth. I asked, with astonishment, what powers Mr. Wallace had, to which he replied, that except to say that Mr. Grattan would receive no hostile message, he had no authority whatever. I expressed my surprise, the rather, as Mr. Grattan was in the first instance about to refer me to a military friend; and at the same time I intimated to Mr. Wallace that the most unpleasant consequences must be the result, it being then my intention to recommend to you a mode of proceeding, which has since been abandoned. He lamented this, but said he had no authority for

going further. Mr. Wallace then stated, that my two last notes to Mr. Grattan were still *unopened;* and offered them to me, but I declined accepting them; the cause assigned for this extraordinary proceeding was, the warmth said to have been evinced by me on the preceding evening; to this I replied, and I am sure that Mr. Wallace will do me the justice to admit, that I was cool upon the occasion, "that if I did any thing wrong, Mr. Grattan was in the possession of my address.

"Your's, my dear Edgeworth, very faithfully,
"JAMES MONTGOMERY.
"To T. N. Edgeworth, Esq. &c."

In the course of Saturday evening the following letter was left at the house of Mr. Grattan:—

"3, Harcourt-place,
"Saturday evening, 15th Sept. 1827.
"Sir—Your having falsely maligned me, in the *Freeman's Journal* newspaper, of which you are the *sworn* Proprietor; and having declined to retract the same, or to render me the satisfaction due to a gentleman; I know of no epithet applicable to you but those of LIBELLER and COWARD; acting under the advice of my friends, I will not condescend to have any recourse to the alternative, in such cases usual, that of inflicting personal chastisement upon the aggressor.
"I am, &c.,
"T. N. EDGEWORTH.
"HENRY GRATTAN, ESQ. M. P."

The following extract from the *Freeman's Journal* of Oct. 19, two years before the challenge was delivered, is calculated to throw some light on this affair.

"We lately thought it incumbent upon us to notice the circumstances of the *Freeman's Journal* being almost universally excluded by the Stamp-office in the selection of newspapers for the insertion of advertisements from that department—an exercise of favouritism altogether inexcusable in the Commissioners of Stamps, knowing, as they must, the superior circulation of the *Freeman's Journal.* We conceive that it is also our duty to expose the like conduct of the Paving Board. We have recently observed in some of the papers, an advertisement, entitled *"Materials for Pavement,"* which has not been sent to the *Freeman's Journal.* We are justified in protesting against this prejudice and partiality. Individuals may be allowed to indulge their private piques and animosities, but no public board, having the expenditure of taxes extracted from the householders of this city, can, without the most flagrant injustice, or without violating their oaths, indulge any personal enmity to the injury of the interests entrusted to their management. We call on the Commissioners of Paving to satisfy the public why the advertisements of that Corporation were taken—and have been withheld for so many years—from the *Freeman's Journal.*

"Could their discontinuance have been occasioned by the necessary and wholesome strictures of this Journal upon certain acts of the Board, in respect to the paving, lighting, and cleansing of the city?

"Is the publication of the advertisements a mere matter of form? If it be, it is only a waste of the public funds to advertise at all. But, if advertisements are useful and necessary—and who will be hardy enough to say they are not—why exclude them from a paper, possessing a circulation greatly beyond that of the *chosen* prints? Government have latterly professed a desire to purify some of our public establishments—and to break up that party and paltry *private* 'management' which brought such deserved discredit on our country. We calculate that in the general improvements, this remnant of *feudal* injustice will not be overlooked.

"We have turned over the catalogue of our offences against the Paving Board without discovering crimes of any great magnitude, save as against Major Taylor, for having pertinaciously insisted that stones should not be imported from Scotland or England, while much better and more durable stones could be had at home, even within a few miles of Dublin. On this monstrous, we had almost said iniquitous importation, we did express our sentiments with considerable indignation."

The *Freeman* of September 20th, 1827, says:—"It would be no doubt interesting to some institutions, and some men, that the press should be gagged, but this paper will not deviate from the line already laid down by its conductors; nor will it be

deterred from exposing public abuses. The matters arising out of
a recent occurrence are now referred to a judicial tribunal. We
are of opinion that the proprietor (Mr. Grattan) has upheld the
liberty of the press, the rights of his injured fellow-citizens, and
the independence of his seat in parliament. He would have been
insane if he had noticed the proceedings in any other manner
than that in which he did. We are of opinion that, if Mr. Grattan
had remained silent on the subject of Local Taxation, and if he
had not night after night, pressed for the production of the
Report of the late Paving Board, we would have witnessed nothing of the late business; Mr. Grattan would never have been
assailed as he has; he never would have been called on to account
(without the delay of a moment) for what he never wrote, never
saw, never knew anything of; and to account (after a declaration
so made) at the pistol mouth. In fact, the original cause of
offence was the conduct of the member in parliament, and the
conduct of this paper in laying before the public these city
abuses. It is remarkable that the paragraph complained of does
not speak of any individual by name, or in terms more severe
than the commissioners of enquiry had done. Now, if Mr.
Grattan was to be fired at for what he never saw and never said,
how does it happen that Mr. Freeman and Mr. Hall, the commissioners, or Alderman Smyth and others, remain unchallenged
and unnoticed? The public will form their opinion upon this.

"In fact, the whole thing is what is called *got up*. The violence
of the proceeding—the party acting, and the *preparation behind
the scenes*, of which we happen to know a little, appear to have
been arranged before Mr. Henry Grattan was waited on by any
individual, or Mr. James Grattan visited by the police. Before all
these absurd, foolish, and empty demonstrations took place, we
were inclined to suspect (to use a nautical phrase) that *there was
something in the wind*. It is fortunate, however, that Mr. Grattan
has not fallen into the snare that was laid for him; and putting
personal bravery (which at best is but an ordinary attribute) out
of the question, we have no doubt that every dispassionate man
will be of opinion, that the course adopted is the best calculated
to vindicate the freedom of the press—to expose public abuses,
and assert the rights of the representative of the people."

The editor says, in another number of *The Freeman,* "We cannot be otherwise than deeply sensible to the independent spirit with which the privileges of the press and its legitimate bounds of responsibility, as attempted lately to be invaded in the person of the proprietor of this paper, have been, and continue to be, vindicated by our contemporaries. From obvious motives, we abstain ourselves from canvassing proceedings, which, were the case not our own, would afford us wide scope for inquiry. Our enlightened brethren of the press have achieved all that we could desire upon this head. In their comments we behold a pure and disinterested estimate of the course which the proprietor of this journal has advisedly pursued, and the view taken of his conduct therein, must be the more gratifying to him, inasmuch as it rather accords with, than influences public opinion. Leaving the case of an individual, about whom we are naturally interested, out of the question, we rejoice at this public expression of sentiment by the press, because it will be a standard for the adjustment of other differences, should the example which it is expected the present will afford, not have the effect of preventing them from arising. We make the following extracts from contemporary journals on the subject of the late transaction.

(FROM THE EVENING POST.)

"We have not the paragraph at which Major Edgeworth took offence before us, but on making some enquires into its nature we are assured,—and not by persons we will say, very friendly to Mr. Grattan, that it is weakness itself, compared with some of the strictures on the conduct of the commissioners which have been made in contemporary journals. We have read the report on the Paving Board, and we do not know that any language which could be used, ought to be considered too severe for the malversations of this Board. But had the paragraph which has given rise to this most inconsiderate proceeding on the part of Major Edgeworth, been all that himself conceived of it, we think Mr. Grattan perfectly right in his refusal to be accountable at the bar of *honor,* for its insertion. Be it remembered, that Major Edgeworth is a public officer; as such, and as such only, was his conduct as well as that of the other commissioners, made the subject matter of comment in Mr. Grattan's paper.

There would be an end of the press, for any useful purposes, if public functionaries, instead of applying to the *law* for redress, should appeal to the pistol. A private libel, in our opinion, should be vindicated in the same manner, but it is only in the circumstances attending such a libel, that even an excuse can be found for the *ultima ratio.*

"We are really sorry on Major Edgeworth's account—sorry for the sake of the highly respectable name he bears—a name which will long illustrate the literature of his country—that he has been so ill advised as to take the course he has followed. But we shall say no more on the subject. We would be peace-makers, if we could, but unfortunately that is now impossible."

(FROM THE MORNING REGISTER.)

"It appears from a statement inserted elsewhere, that in conse-quence of some observations published lately in the *Freeman's Journal,* on Paving Board transactions, Mr. Henry Grattan, the proprietor of that paper, received a hostile message from Major Edgeworth, and declined accepting it. The whole case is not told, and the statement, so far as it goes, is *ex parte;* but it is easily to be inferred, that in the course taken by Mr. Grattan, he was not without advice, and that he acted from feelings of public duty. We conceive ourselves bound to express what occurs to our own mind on the subject—and our opinion decidedly is, that the honorable member was governed by sound counsel, and that he manifested a just sense of the obligations he owed to the press and to society. A wager, they say, is a bad mode of deciding an argument, and a pistol cannot be preferable. Mr. Edgeworth may shoot Mr. Grattan, and still be (what we are very far from considering him) the greatest villain in existence. But if the *duello* could decide any thing in the present case, the interests, we will not say of the press, but of the public, would not permit us to tolerate an appeal to its arbitration. Mr. Grattan's paper, in animadverting on the conduct of individuals connected with the Board, discharged an imperative, and, we have no doubt, a painful public duty. It acted as the advocate in a Court of Justice; as the judicial functionary on the bench; or as the representative of the people in the senate. There is no argument that could be advanced, to show the right of a person, situated as Major Edgeworth is, to challenge Mr. Grattan to the field, that would not warrant a party to call upon the first magistrate in the state to answer with his life for conduct pursued by him in the honest and conscientious discharge of a solemn public duty."

"We dare say the public will trouble themselves little in pursuing inquiries as to the reputation for personal courage as is involved in the present transaction. There can be no doubt of the *pluck* of the parties. Major Edgeworth is, they say, the devil at a pistol. We have no doubt that he can "box his corner" in that way as well as another; but we believe he has done nothing more like an *amateur* at the art than what has been performed by the object of his present anger. The son of the immortal Grattan could not be a person easily deterred from the pursuit of a course which real honor or duty would prescribe.

"On the whole, then, we can have no hesitation in saying that what appears on the face of the commissioners report, warranted *The Freeman* in a great latitude of observation."

(FROM THE PATRIOT.)

"As for Mr. Grattan, he acted as he ought to have done; and we are happy to find that it fell to the lot of a person of his high character and tried courage to vindicate the legitimate privileges of the press, attempted to be invaded in his person. Were the editor of this paper placed in the same circumstances, he would act in a similar manner, and in doing so, would fulfil, as he conceives, his duty to the press and to the public. Did he indeed make an attack upon private life, or impute gross criminality even to public men, without documentary evidence to sustain him, he would consider his own conduct incorrect, and the man he maligned entitled to atonement. But as long as that is not the case—as long as the press confined itself to the legitimate discussion of the conduct of public men, and the *Freeman* did no more—as long as that discussion is founded upon documents given to the public by authority, which was the case of the Paving Report; so long that press should not submit to have the rights of public discussion invaded by personal responsibility for the discharge of public duty: and the principal which would oblige the journalist to risk his life for every exercise of his duty, would tend to give impunity to every public functionary who chose to fight in order to silence the voice of public complaint."

"Most of our contemporaries have copied from the *Dublin Evening Mail,* a long advertisement from Major Edgeworth, one of the Commissioners of the Old Paving Board, in Dublin, who complains of some remarks made by the Dublin *Freeman's Journal,* of which paper Henry Grattan, Esq. M.P. is proprietor, and of the refusal of Mr. Grattan to give Mr. Edgeworth satisfaction in what is considered the indispensable mode of settling disputes in the sister country. Without at all entering into the merits of the first part of the complaint made by Mr. Edgeworth, as to the truth or falsehood of the observations which have given him offence, farther than expressing our opinion, that a paper so respectable and well-conducted as the *Freeman's Journal,* is not likely to give offence without cause, we must declare, that we think Mr. Grattan acts wisely and properly in refusing to indulge with powder and ball recreation, every gentleman who may fancy himself aggrieved by articles which appear in the paper of which he may be the proprietor. The laws of the country are open to Major Edgeworth; and as judges and juries have generally a horror of libel—a horror in some cases almost approaching to the ludicrous—there can be little doubt that he would obtain all the redress that his case deserves. To the laws only ought he to appeal; and we think Mr. Grattan displays true courage in braving the epithets which his refusal to afford Mr. Edgeworth the chance of blowing out his brains, for an offence of which individually he is probably as innocent as the Emperor of China, has produced from his challenger. Major Edgeworth, after bestowing the very *gentlemanly* epithets of 'libeller and coward' upon Mr. Grattan, says, 'acting under the advice of my friends, I will not condescend to have recourse to the alternative in such cases usual—that of inflicting personal chastisement upon the aggressor.' Mr. Edgeworth acts very prudently in following this advice of his friends—there would not only be disgrace in the attempt to inflict personal chastisement where none is due, but there might also be danger in it;

for, although we know little of the comparative physical powers of the two gentlemen, we believe Mr. Grattan is not the man to submit to a horsewhipping from Mr. Edgeworth, although he may bear in silence the insult which is lavished upon him for his refusal to accept the challenge of a person who has no reasonable ground for offering it, considering that the course, in a case like his, is otherwise marked out both by custom and gentlemanly feelings."

(FROM THE MORNING CHRONICLE.)

"Some remarks made in the Dublin *Freeman's Journal,* of which Mr. Grattan is the proprietor, on the conduct of Major Edgeworth, in his capacity of Member of a Board, which, like all other public bodies in Ireland, seems to have lived by plunder, has led to a hostile correspondence."

The following is an extract from a letter which we published on the subject in the Dublin *Morning Post,* and we had the satisfaction of discovering that it afforded general satisfaction at the period:—

"As the author of the Royal Code of Honor, which has been sanctioned by the highest authorities in Europe, I request your prompt co-operation in the establishment of a Court of Honor, for the examination of such cases as that which has so recently occurred.

"An appeal to such a court, in the case of Mr. Bric, would have saved the life of a fellow citizen, for it would have instantly recommended that very trifling reparation, which a few hasty words between the zealous partizans, Messrs. Hutchinson and Callaghan, demanded.

"In the recent case, a Court of Honor might be called upon to say—

"1st. Whether the proprietor or editor of a paper is responsible for examining with freedom the conduct of a public body or a public man?

"2d. Who is responsible to the laws of honor—the gentleman who owns a paper, or the editor by whom it is conducted?

"I have collected several hundred duelling cases, and I recollect but one, in which a proprietor who had an editor, assumed responsibility at the hazard of his life. That was the case in which

Mr. Barron gratuitously became responsible for the article of a correspondent, which article was not submitted to his Editor.

"The case of Messrs. Barron and Sargent was another of those which might have been adjusted by a court of honor. Such a court would not have justified eight shots between two persons who gratuitously placed themselves in the shoes of a father and a clergyman.

"I shall be happy to record the names of such professional and private gentlemen as may be willing to act upon a court of honor, upon any future case, and have the honor to be, a friend to the freedom of the press, as well as of courtesy in its indulgence.

"JOSEPH HAMILTON.

"Annadale Cottage, near Dublin."

Previous to the Waterford election in 1826, the writers for the Mail and Chronicle too frequently forgot "to magnify their office," and descended to great personalities in their attempts to depreciate the characters of their political opponents. A singular case of responsibility occurred on this occasion, which involved the proprietor of the Chronicle in a duel, and we place the facts on record in these pages not so much because we were most intimately connected with them all, as for the purpose of guarding other editors against a usurpation of their pens by occasional auxiliaries, who may possibly involve them in unexpected difficulties.

On Saturday, the 1st. of April, 1826, an *apparently* editorial article was published in the Chronicle, in consequence of which Mr. Richard Sargent posted the following notice in the Commercial coffee-room on Monday morning:—

"The *Chronicle* of Saturday last, in an article alluding to several magistrates of the county of Waterford, has grossly slandered my father; I thus publicly proclaim the author of that article to be a LIAR and a SCOUNDREL; whether or no I am entitled to add COWARD, will depend upon the notice he may take of this publication. If he has any remaining pretension to the character of a gentleman, he will give his name; if not I shall take no farther notice of any anonymous publication."

This notice led to the following correspondence, and to a very desperate duel:—

TO THE EDITOR OF THE WATERFORD CHRONICLE.
"Rathculliheen, April 5, 1826.

"Sir,—As the course which Mr. Richard Sargent has thought proper to adopt, in consequence of a certain paragraph which he considered as reflecting on the character of his father, Mr. Alderman Sargent (and which appeared in the Waterford Chronicle of Saturday last), has obtained considerable notoriety, and lest it may be supposed that the notice posted by Mr. Sargent contained any *allusion* to Mr. Barron, I beg your insertion of the following correspondence:—

MR. WYSE TO MR. MORRIS. NO. 1.

"SIR,—Having called on Mr. Sargent, as the friend of Mr. Barron, Mr. Sargent has directed me to you, for any explanation which I may require; I in consequence beg to know, if in the placard or notice which was this day posted, any *allusion* was intended to be made *directly* or *indirectly,* to Mr. Barron.

"I have the honor to be, &c. &c.
"FRANCIS WYSE.
"*Commercial Hotel, April* 3, 1826.
"To Richard Wall Morris, Esq. &c. &c."

MR. MORRIS' ANSWER. NO. 1.

"SIR,—In reply to your note of the third of April instant (marked No. 1,) I have to state, that I must refer you to the notice which Mr. Sargent posted in the coffee-room, for the answer of your question, who the person was to whom Mr. Sargent alluded—it being therein distinctly stated to be the author of the paragraph which appeared in the *New Waterford Chronicle* of Saturday last, in which allusion was made, I need not say in what terms, to his father, Mr. Alderman Sargent.

"Sir, I have the honor to be, &c. &c.
"RICHARD W. MORRIS.
"Waterford, April 3, Monday-night, 11 o'clock."

MR. WYSE TO MR. MORRIS. NO. 2.

"SIR,—I beg to acknowledge your note in reply to my last, No. 1, and to remind you, that the question proposed by me was not '*who the person was to whom Mr. Sargent alluded*' in his placard or notice, posted in the Commercial News-room; but if any allusion was intended, directly or indirectly, to Mr. Barron?

"This query I consider to be a plain and a simple one, the

responsibility of answering which, I am sure Mr. Sargent cannot wish to shrink from by any evasion. I again repeat the question— 'If, in the placard or notice, which was this day posted in the Commercial News-room, any allusion was intended, directly or indirectly, to Mr. Barron?'

"I wait your reply, and have the honor to be, Sir, your obedient servant,

"Francis Wyse,

"Commercial Hotel, April 3.

"To Richard Wall Morris, Esq."

Mr. Morris's Answer. No. 2.

"Sir,—I have before me your note marked No. 2. As friend to Mr. Sargent, I have only to reply to you by stating, that I do not feel myself called upon to say, whether any particular individual be alluded to or not, unless that individual declares himself to be the author of the paragraph which appeared in the *Chronicle* of Saturday last. I must again repeat what I have so often expressed verbally to you, that to me it appears most strange that such very great difficulty should be made in arranging this affair, as my friend Mr. Sargent has so explicitly expressed himself in the notice he posted. I have the honour to be, Sir, your obedient servant,

"Richard W. Morris.

"To F. Wyse, Esq."   "*Waterford, April 3.*

Mr. Wyse to Mr. Morris. No. 3.

"Sir,—I have just received your last, marked No. 2. and beg to say that Mr. Barron does not consider himself called upon, nor will he afford Mr. Sargent the satisfaction to learn whether *he is* or *is not* the author of the paragraph which appeared in the *Chronicle* of Saturday last, and to which Mr. Sargent has been pleased to allude in his placard, posted in the Commercial-room this day.

"But on the part of Mr. Barron, I feel myself called upon to say, that if *any possible allusion* was intended to Mr. Barron in the 'placard' in question, I am prepared, on the part of my friend, to demand such further explanation from Mr. Sargent as the nature of the circumstances may require. I shall await your final answer until 12 o'clock to-morrow.

"I have the honor to be, Sir, your obedient servant,

"Francis Wyse,

"*Commercial Hotel, April* 3, 1826.

"To R. W. Morris, Esq."

Mr. Wyse, to prevent the transaction, until its termination, becoming public, addressed the following to Mr. Morris:—

"Sir,—Lest the affair between Mr. Barron and Mr. Sargent should gain publicity, I beg to acquaint you, that on our part it will not be mentioned to a single individual; it will therefore rest with you to see that it does not become matter of public notice till terminated.

"I have the honor to be, Sir, your obedient humble servant,

"FRANCIS WYSE.

"To R. W. Morris, Esq. the Mall. *April* 3."

MR. MORRIS'S ANSWER. NO. 3.

"SIR,—If I rightly understood you in your verbal communication last night, you distinctly stated that Mr. Philip Barron is the proprietor of the *Waterford Chronicle.* If I misunderstood you I request you will set me right on this point. But assuming that Mr. P. Barron is the proprietor, and considering that he refuses to afford Mr. Sargent the satisfaction of saying whether he is or is not the author of the paragraph in question, Mr. Sargent considers himself entitled to attach to the proprietor all those responsibilities which the author, if known, must have incurred.

"I have only to add, that if the nature of our communications shall acquire publicity, it will not be through my means, or those of my friend, Mr. Sargent.

"I have the honor to be, &c.   "R. W. MORRIS.

"*The Mall, 4th. April,* 1826.

"To Francis Wyse, Esq."

MR. WYSE TO MR. MORRIS. NO. 5.

"SIR,—I need not say that I was much surprised on receiving your letter of this day's date. I beg to remind you that it was expressly agreed upon, that all communication relating to the affair between Mr. Barron and Mr. Sargent should be in writing; consequently must refer you to my letters, 1, 2, 3, and 4, which I presume are yet in your possession, in any of which I do not recollect to have alluded to Mr. Barron as the proprietor of the *Waterford Chronicle;* I consider you, therefore, as having assumed a new ground, which I cannot possibly recognise.

"When Mr. Sargent subscribed his name to the document in question, he must have known whether he intended any *allusion* to Mr. Barron or not.

"The question, therefore, to which I have required an answer, and which I again repeat for the *last* time, is simply—

"*If in the placard or notice which was this day (Monday) posted in the Commercial news-room, any allusion was intended, directly or indirectly, to Mr. Barron?*

"To this I must request your *direct* answer, which I shall expect by three o'clock this day.

"I have the honor to be, Sir, your obedient servant,

"FRANCIS WYSE.

"*Packet Hotel, William Street,* 2 *o'clock, April* 4.

"To Richard W. Morris, Esq. the Mall."

MR. MORRIS' REPLY.

"SIR,—The notice posted by Mr. Sargent did not contain any allusion whatever. It was a distinct and unequivocal charge against the author of the publication which gave him offence, not one word of which Mr. Sargent will retract.

"I concur in opinion with you that all *correspondence* on the subject should here terminate. I shall remain at home for one hour.

"I have the honor to be, Sir, your obedient humble servant,

"RICHARD W. MORRIS.

"*Half-past three, Tuesday.*

"To Francis Wyse, Esq. &c."

MR. WYSE TO MR. MORRIS. NO. 6.

"SIR,—On behalf of Mr. Barron I beg to say, that I feel perfectly satisfied with the explanation afforded in your last note.

"I have the honor to be,

"Your obedient servant,

"FRANCIS WYSE.

"To Richard W. Morris, Esq. the Mall."

Thus has terminated this affair.

"Mr. Barron originally required to know whether the notice was intended to convey any *allusion* to him; and Mr. Sargent has at length declared that "*the notice did* NOT *contain any allusion whatever.*

"I have the honor to be, Sir, &c.

"FRANCIS WYSE.

"*Rathculliheen April* 5*th,* 1826."

"Mr. Barron not choosing to give any satisfaction as to *his being, or not being,* the author of the paragraph in question, and having determined not to disavow it until all allusion to him was distinctly disclaimed—now that he is not called upon to do so, feels no hesitation in saying that he was *not* the author, and has little doubt that the identity and real character of the author were very well known throughout this city.

"Mr. Barron also avows himself the proprietor of the *Waterford Chronicle.*"

We have extracted thus far from the *Chronicle* of Thursday, which then gives a long letter from the Rev. John Sheehan, avowing himself the author of the offensive statement of the preceding Saturday, and maintaining its correctness.

Tuesday afternoon, Mr. Barron was bound over by a magistrate of the county and city of Waterford. Mr. Sargent was sought for the same purpose, but was not found.

Thursday the following notice was posted in the Commercial Coffee-room:—

"I fully approve of the publication of the correspondence which passed between Mr. Francis Wyse, on the part of Mr. Philip Barron, and Mr. Richard Wall Morris, on my part; and, had Mr. Barron and his friend stopped there, and left the public to form their own unbiassed judgment, and thus terminated this affair, it should not have been revived by me. But Mr. Wyse has thought proper to add his own interpretation; and Mr. P. Barron, who is at last avowed to be the proprietor of the *Chronicle,* has further added an ungentlemanly commentary. Mr. R. Morris, in his letter No. 3, distinctly stated that I, considering Mr. Barron as the proprietor of the *Chronicle,* attached to him *(as such)* all the responsibilities of authorship, until authorship should be disavowed by him. Mr. Wyse's letter in reply, No. 5, manifestly avoided the responsibility which *I sought to attach to Mr. Barron, as proprietor,* and I became apprehensive that, if I continued to apply myself to him in that capacity, measures of a different kind would have been resorted to. I, therefore, in Mr. Morris's next letter, waved the doubtful term of 'allusion,' and renewed in the strongest possible language my original charge against the author, fully expecting that Mr. Barron would have taken upon himself the responsibility of authorship, though he declined that of

ownership; and certainly not at all expecting that he would have
resorted to the miserable subterfuge of shifting the responsibility
on an irresponsible clergyman.

"RICHARD SARGENT.

"Lady-lane, April 6, 1826."

The *Chronicle* gave the following description of the duel
which afterwards took place between these gentlemen:—

"A hostile meeting took place yesterday morning. The call proceeded from Mr. Barron. The two principals, accompanied each
by his friend, and each by a professional gentleman, left this
something before three in the morning, and fought a little before
six, about half a mile at this side of Ballyhale, in the county of
Kilkenny, about thirteen miles from Waterford. Each fired three
ineffectual shots, and each missed fire once, Mr. Barron at the
second, Mr. Sargent at the fourth discharge. Mr. Wyse declared
that his friend was satisfied, and the parties returned to town.
They arrived here at a quarter before nine."

The editor, whose statement at the time was gratuitously circulated through Waterford, having in vain expostulated against
the introduction of abusive letters, and especially against abusive articles, from irresponsible pens, in the editorial language,
sent the following advertisement for the Waterford Mirror of
April the 3:—

"The individual who was thrice invited down from Dublin, to
conduct the *New Waterford Chronicle,* is too familiar with his
own infirmities to exercise an uncharitable censorship on others;
yet he is unwilling to appear responsible, even for a single item
which belongs not to his account, lest he should be supposed to
have deviated from his peaceful habits.

"He never wrote nor sanctioned an offending sentence, line, or
paragraph, respecting any individual, since that journal has commenced. He embarked in what he thought a generous warfare
against narrow systems; but to his fellow-man, and even to his bit-
terest adversary, he brought a healing not an irritating spirit.

"The publication of the various editorial articles which have
been suppressed at the proprietor's desire, would have lessened
the necessity for the present declaration of his editor.

"Were the objects of the latter merely to increase the comforts of an interesting family, by preserving a situation which depended upon another person's will, he might with great convenience and facility have sacrificed 'the right' in pursuit of 'the expedient,' and occupied an advantageous position in the warfare of the pens; but he is solicitous for other interests which he cannot compromise, and he remembers with an indescribable delight, that in James Montgomery, of the *Sheffield Iris*, were united the editor, the gentleman, the patriot, and the Christian.

"The office of the editor has been inconsiderately invaded; but he can assure the respectable body of which he is a very humble member, that the rights and spirits of the corps have not been wholly unasserted.

"When the young gentleman, who is the proprietor of the *Chronicle*, shall have acquired all those advantages which time alone can furnish, he must perceive that it is his interest, as it is unquestionably is his duty, to preserve from violation every editorial right.

"4, Henrietta-street, Waterford April 2, 1826."

Within a few months afterwards the last paragraph was literally fulfilled. Mr. Barron, a young man, who commenced his literary labours with great public support, and nearly one thousand pounds a year, announced the death of his paper, and his compulsory exile from a country in which he wished to live and to expire; bowed down by civil actions and by criminal informations, for invading individual character, he saw his error when too late. In a single action which was tried at Cork, a verdict for £1,350, with costs, was given against him, after enduring all the severity of opposing counsel, and offering in vain to publish any apology which the plaintiff might dictate. He had been told in the presence of his cousin the very day on which the letter was written which produced the duel, that his conduct to his editor would fall on him and his establishment, and so indeed it did, affording to every proprietor of a public journal, an awful admonition, not to attempt invasion of the editorial rights, to adopt or to reject the writings and suggestions of all his correspondents, and to act like a responsible minister to an irresponsible sovereign.

The editor, whose repeated admonitions Mr. Barron had unfor-

tunately slighted, was one of the most uncompromising patriots of
his age and nation; and of whose abilities and conduct, his political
and literary adversaries have given the most honorable testimonials; yet the following singular passage has proceeded from his pen.
"May every scribe be well instructed in the best of policy (Mat. xiii.
52), and continually emulous to magnify his enviable office, (Rom.
xi. 13)—may neither the inkhorn at his side, (Ezek. ix. 2,) nor the
sharp thrashing instrument with teeth, in his right hand, (Isa. xli.
13, 15,) tend to maculate his alb, or to disqualify him for the honors of that approaching period, in which the teachers of the million
(Dan. xii. 3), shall be eternally illumed, like stars in the re-united
coronets of Israel and Judah—a period, in which it is asserted that
the great dispenser of all power, shall raise up at least one faithful
scribe to be a profitable ruler (Eccles. x. 4, 5, 14.)" Whether his
political theology be correct or otherwise, we shall not now
enquire; but conclude the present article in our wishful language,
as a writer, a patriot, and a citizen of the world. May neither malice, interest, nor affection, degrade THE MAJESTY OF THE PRESS—
and may its corrective domination be increased, until ALL POWER-
FUL TRUTH shall have ceased to be a libel.

RESPONSIBILITY OF THE BAR

"To wrong the wronger, and to right the right."

Much of what has been said in the preceding article may be applied to gentlemen who are engaged as advocates in courts of equity or law. No pecuniary consideration whatever should induce a member of that honorable body to state what is not fact, and what may have a tendency to affect the reputation, life, or property of the person against whom he is employed to plead. The man who can hire himself to be the assassin of a character, possesses the disposition, though he may want the courage and the fee to assassinate the owner of that character, and must often be exposed to that coarse personal collision out of court, which the feelings of a harassed suitor may dictate. If, however, the advocate have a just occasion to expose a fraud, conspiracy, or oppressive action, he should fearlessly perform his duty, and with firmness refuse the gauntlet of the individual whom he may oppose. In our Bar Quarrels we shall have many cases illustrative of this head, at present we shall mention one which excited general sympathy at New York. The son of the Spanish consul, a fine young man at the American bar, was engaged as counsel against a Mr. Goodwin, the acknowledged owner of an American privateer, and the alledged contriver of a piratical expedition. The barrister in the discharge of what he thought his duty, incurred the strong resentment of Mr. Goodwin, who challenged him repeatedly to fight, which was declined both from conscientious motives, and a determination to support the independence of the bar. Goodwin followed his assailant into Broadway where he spat upon him in the presence of some ladies with whom he had been walking, and with one of whom he was upon the very eve of marriage. Having been called

by several injurious and tantalizing epithets he forgot the defer-
ence he owed to his trembling female friends, and his
respectable profession. He drew a cane sword, Goodwin drew
another, and the barrister fell dead upon the spot. So strong was
the popular resentment against Mr. Goodwin, that to preserve
him from a summary punishment by the inhabitants of New
York, he was obliged to be concealed in a private apartment of
the prison.

RESPONSIBILITY OF
PUBLIC FUNCTIONARIES

"The man, resolv'd and steady to his trust,
Inflexible to ill, and obstinately just,
May the rude rabble's insolence despise."

For the conscientious discharge of a public or a professional duty, no individual should condescend to meet a challenger. It would have been absurd in Judge Gascoigne to have quit the bench in order to fight a duel with his sovereign's heir. His conduct was more dignified, and the submission of Prince Henry becoming that illustrious transgressor of decorum.

An experienced officer, who commanded at the Magazines, near Liverpool, having received a challenge for offending a young gentleman while he was in the correct discharge of his official duties, sent the following answer:—

"SIR,—Your challenge is now before me, and shall speedily be behind your very humble servant, &c."

The following excellent letter has been copied from the New York Gazette, and is worthy of extensive publication. The Hon. David Barton, a senator from Missouri, in the discharge of his duty before the committee on public lands, made some remarks which were offensive to Henry W. Conway, a delegate from Arkansas. Mr. C. without much ceremony, sent Mr. Barton a challenge by his friend Major Miller, under date of Washington, the 27th ult. To which we subjoin the answer of the same date:—

"Sir,—Your letter of this evening, dated 27th June, 1824, has been just received by Major Miller.

"The offensive expressions in my letter of the 5th of May, are not only true, but proved by me to be so, in the course of my public duties in arraigning the official conduct of your uncle, and yourself, as his deputy, for which I refer all concerned to the records of the nation contained in the testimony by me filed in that case, and to the able report of the Attorney-General of the United States upon that subject.

"I therefore decline the honour proposed by you, never intending to recognise the principle, that the investigation of official conduct, whether of principal or deputy, in the manner in which I have conducted the one in question, can impose any obligation to give the kind of satisfaction which you seem to desire, even to an innocent party.

"I also remind you, that my letter of the 5th May last. Was elicited by a document filed by you in your own case and that of your uncle, giving a most erroneous representation of my motives and conduct in the investigation alluded to. This closes our correspondence.

> "Your obedient,
> "David Barton.

"H. W. Conway, Esq."

Mr. Charles Dawson had been employed by Sir A. Hart, the Irish chancellor, to enquire professionally into the property of Mr. Watson, a barrister who had proposed for Miss Elizabeth Martha Hart. The lover in a letter, charged Dawson with having made misrepresentations of the state of his property in order to obstruct the marriage, and called him a liar for his falsehood, and a villain for lending himself to such a purpose; that unless Dawson meant to shield himself by his cowardice from the consequences of his conduct, he must give the defendant a meeting at *Calais*. For sending this challenge he was fined £300. and imprisoned two months.

In January, 1823, at a public meeting at Kilmainham, our late worthy friend, Mr. John Burne, the King's counsel, "stated that there was no person connected with the Irish government on whom Lord Wellesley could depend but Mr. Plunkett." A Dublin paper asserts "that shortly after the meeting, Mr. B. received a visit from the S——r G——l. Much conversation of rather a cool and argumentative kind, grounded on the report of Mr. B.'s speech, that appeared in the papers, was the consequence. The S——r G——l pointed to certain expressions, and pressed Mr. B. to avow or disavow them. This Mr. B. declined doing, upon the ground that his compliance would recognize a right in every clerk at the castle, to call upon him for the explanation of phrases, not specially applied to any individual—and would, besides, involve what he should consider an infringement of the freedom of discussion. The S——r-General departed, giving Mr. B. reason to conclude that the affair had not terminated. In some time afterwards Mr. B. received a visit from Mr. S——n, when a conversation ensued similar in tendency and result to that which had before taken place. At the departure of this gentleman, Mr. B. intimated, as the matter was still unsettled, that he would be prepared, by a particular time, to appoint a gentleman to confer with Mr. S——n, and make any arrangement which might appear expedient or necessary.—This intimation drew from Mr. S——n an observation, that Mr. B. was not to understand that he had yet come to any definite course of proceeding—and that Mr. B. might expect again to see him. In a short time Mr. S——n paid a second visit, and closed the conferences by announcing, that his friend did not think himself called upon to proceed further, as Mr. B. declined explanation on the ground that compliance would, in his mind, involve a surrender of the freedom of discussion."

We mention the fact as being highly honorable to Mr. Solicitor General J—y, whose worth and courage, are equal to his high professional station and attainments, and who has scarcely ever yet been known to violate that courtesy which is so essential to the reputation of a gentleman.

The freedom of discussion should be carefully preserved. All public functionaries, from the judge or senator down to the humblest witness in the box, should discharge their duties without malice or affection, and despise the man who would attempt to hold them personally responsible for their due performance. All speakers and writers should, however, be habitually abstinent in the use of all unnecessary and injurious verbiage, and as some of them, whom we could name, appear too busy for reflection, we shall close the present article with our reflections upon slander.

Slander is one of the most ungenerous, unprofitable, wanton, and malicious crimes to which human nature is capable of descending; it has been equally reprobated by the Christian and Pagan moralist, and is hostile to the laws of our nation, our nature, and our God. It is asserting in the absence of another that which is false and disreputable. If the lie be of our own creation, we are responsible for all the mischief it occasions, though perhaps we are deprived of the ability to heal the wounds which we inflict. If it originate with others, and we contribute to its currency, it becomes the child of our adoption, and we are partners in the turpitude. Like a tyger loosed amidst a flock of lambs, it eludes the pursuit of its neglectful keeper, who, endeavouring to regain, must trace it by the carnage in its course; so extensive is the operation of this detestable vice, that even in the hour of repentance and anxiety for atonement, though the victim may forgive, the mischief cannot be entirely discontinued.

A man's good name is frequently his support, perhaps that of his family, and some helpless object of his protective hospitality; to many it is far more dear than life; to most persons it is more valuable than riches. A writer who has the reputation of being familiar with human feeling, says,

> "He who filches from me my good name,
>   Robs me of that which not enriches him,
>   And makes me poor indeed."

As it is most cowardly to smite a man behind, or to fire upon an unsuspecting person from a thicket, so it is to abuse a man in so tender a point as reputation; it is unjust to condemn without strong evidence of guilt, or affording the accused the common privilege of defence; and it is unchristian-like to do that to others which we would not wish they should do to us. How contemptible is the situation of the slanderer when confronted with the victim of his malice, and driven to the cowardly subterfuge of softening or denying his words, or perhaps transferring the odium of their coinage to some person who is absent.

We are told that the slanderer's tongue deviseth mischief like a sharp razor, working deceitfully, (Psm. liii. 2, 3;) that he loves evil more than good, and lying rather than to speak righteousness. In Psalm ci. 5, is a resolution to cut off such as privily slander their neighbour; and in Psalm xv. it is declared, that he who slanders, reproaches, or even takes up a reproach against his neighbour shall not ascend into the hill of the Lord.

We are told in Proverbs xxvi. that as the fire goes out where there is no wood to feed it, so strife is discontinued where there is no tale-bearer; and St. James declares in chapter iii. that there is a world of iniquity in this crime; that its root is in hell, from whence it brings up flames to set on fire the very course of nature. Slander is in direct opposition to that charity of the Gospel which is the distinguishing emblem of the real Christian, (John xiii.); a virtue possessed by those individuals who have been born of God, (1. John iii.); and without which no good work can be available, (1 Cor. xiii.) A Christian should speak evil of no man, (Tit. iii. 2); have a charitable hope respecting every man, (I Cor. xii.); lay aside all malice, envy, and evil speaking, (1. Peter ii.); love his neighbour fervently, with a pure heart, (1. Peter i.); love him as himself, and as a member of the same spiritual body, (Romans xii.)

If slander in general be so great a crime, how much more wicked is it to create dissentions between friends, kindred, or persons who are happily cemented by the laws of wedlock; to traduce the friends of virtue, or persons who live but to achieve good actions.

QUARRELS ABOUT LADIES

"And hearts that glow'd with lawless love,
Were chill'd by lawless steel."

Lord C—— having prevailed upon the wife of Mr. Blisset, a merchant, to elope with him, was overtaken in the street by the enraged husband with a sword. "Villain," said the merchant, "leave the wanton and defend yourself." "To increase your rage," said his lordship, "learn that I have been familiar with your wife these twelve months." They engaged in the street. The first pass was fatal to the nobleman, the sword of his adversary having passed through his heart. The survivor, after throwing his bloody weapon into the Thames, escaped on board a fishing-smack to Helvoet-fluys, where he entered into the military service.

Villiers, Duke of Buckingham, not contented with having seduced the Countess of Shrewsbury, and publishing her fall, took every possible opportunity of provoking the much injured Earl to a single combat, hoping that he should find a very easy conquest, as his lordship was a quiet, puny, and inoffensive man. The Duke insulted him upon all occasions; and at last declared in public, that there was no glory in c——g Lord Shrewsbury, who had not the spirit to resent the injury. This last insult was not overlooked, the Earl sent him a message, and they agreed to fight at Barn-Elms, in presence of two gentlemen whom they selected as their seconds. The principals and seconds engaged at the same time. The first thrust was fatal to the Earl of Shrewsbury, and his friend killed the Duke's second with equal expedition. Buckingham much elated with this exploit, set out immediately to the Earl's seat at Cleifden, where he boasted of the murder, and shewed the blood upon his sword as a recommendation to the affections of an unworthy widow. Yet this same

duke was a cowardly poltroon, as will be evident from the following case.

The Duke of Buckingham and the Earl of Ossory having
quarrelled, the Earl challenged Buckingham to meet him privately in Chelsea fields; but the Duke crossed the river Thames
to Battersea, where he pretended to wait for Ossory, and then
proceeded to the House of Lords, where he complained that the
Earl, after giving him the rendezvous, had been unfaithful to his
appointment. He thought the house would interfere in the pre-
vention of the duel, and was not much in error, for their lord-
ships made both the disputants pledge their honor that the
quarrel should proceed no further.

One of the commentators upon Pope asserts, that the
Countess, in the habit of a page, held the Duke's horse during
the combat with Lord Shrewsbury.

The possessions of the Duke passed to the Duncombe family.
By his great dissipation he wasted his immense inheritance, and
died in extreme want and misery, upon the 15th of April, 1687, at
a house in Kirby Moorside. The page of an old tattered register-
book belonging to the parish, simply records his burial; but in
what part of the hallowed ground his remains were deposited is
unknown. The following is a literal copy of the register—
"Burials, 1687, April 17th, Gorges vilaus Lord dooke of booking-
ham." The Earl of Arran, who was accidentally passing through
Kirby Moorside, attended the Duke in his last moments, and
being obliged to pursue his journey, he gave directions for the
funeral. The following lines of Pope have a reference to the
debaucheries and death of this unfortunate peer.

> "In the worst inn's worst room, with mat half hung,
> The floors of plaster, and the walls of dung,
> On once a flock bed, but repaired with straw,
> With tape-tied curtains never meant to draw,
> The George and Garter dangling from that bed,
> Where tawdry yellow strove with dirty red,
> Great Villiers lies—alas! how changed from him;
> That life of pleasure, and that soul of whim!
> Gallant and gay in Cliefden's proud alcove,
> The bower of wanton Shrewsbury and love."

The Duke exhibited a most melancholy instance of the prostitution of brilliant talents; and the whole business of his life was the gratification of the most sensual appetites. His character has been strikingly delineated by Zimri, in Dryden's Absalom and Achitophel. By a letter to Dr. Barrow, which will be found in page 402 of the History of Scarborough, the Duke appears to have had a hearty, though a late conviction of his errors.

The following laconic correspondence has recently got abroad among the upper circles, to the great annoyance of a female of high fashion who is known to be the subject of it; the words we have put in italics are underscored in the originals:—

"Saturday, July 17.

"Lord —— is *given to understand* that Sir W—— has affirmed in a public company that Lady —— was a person of *doubtful character.* Lord —— requests to be informed whether Sir W—— did make such assertion, and if he did, begs to ask for an explanation of it. The bearer will wait for his answer."

ANSWER.

"Sir W—— does not recollect to have used the expression referred to respecting the character of Lady ——, nor does he think it likely he should, as he does not know any female in the circle of fashion of whose character *there can be less doubt.*"

The duel between Mr. Scott, afterwards Lord Clonmel, and Mr. Cuffe, afterwards Lord Tyrawley, was caused and attended by circumstances which combine to form a curious narrative. Lady Tyrawley had an utter dislike for her husband (then the Honorable James Cuffe). They had no children; and she made various efforts to induce him to consent to a distinct and total separation. There being no substantial cause for such a measure, Mr. Cuffe looked upon it as ridiculous, and would not consent. At length the lady hit upon an excellent mode for carrying her wishes into effect, and ensuring a separate maintenance, but I have never heard of the precedent being followed. Barrington says:—

"Mr. Cuffe found her one day in tears, a thing not frequent with her ladyship, who had a good deal of the amazon about her.

She sobbed—threw herself on her knees—went through the usual evolutions of a repentant female—and at length told her husband that she was unworthy of his protection—had been faithless to him, and was a lost and guilty woman. I suppose there is a routine of contrition, explanation, rage, horror, &c. which generally attends developments of this nature; and I take for granted, that the same was duly performed by the Honorable Mr. and Mrs. Cuffe. Suffice it to say, that the latter was put into a sedan chair, and ordered out of the house forthwith to private lodgings, until it was the will of her injured lord to send a deed of annuity for her support. Mr. Cuffe next proceeded to a common friend, and informed him that his wife had owned "that villain Scott," the Attorney-General, and the pretended friend of his family, to be her seducer! that not his love but his honour was so deeply concerned, as to render the death of one or the other necessary: and without further ceremony, a message was sent, for mortal combat, to the Attorney-General, urging the lady's confession, his own dishonorable breach of trust, and Mr. Cuffe's determination to fight him.

"Mr. Scott well-knowing that a declaration of innocence would, by the world, be considered either as an honorable perjury on his part to save Mrs. Cuffe's reputation, or as a mode of screening himself from her husband's vengeance, and in no case be believed, even by the good-natured part of society, made up his mind for the worst. The husband and supposed gallant accordingly met, and exchanged shots; each party having heard the bullets humanely whiz past his ears, without indicating a desire of becoming more intimately acquainted. Mr. Scott told his antagonist that he was totally mistaken, and gave his honor that he never had the slightest familiarity with the lady, who he concluded must have lost her reason. There was no cause for denying credence to this, whilst, on the other hand, it was but too likely that Mr. Cuffe had been tricked by his lady wife. She was sure of a separation, for he had turned her out; and if he had fallen on the field of honor, she had a noble jointure; so that she was *in utrumque parata*, secure under every chance.

"On his return he sent her a severe reprimand; and announced but a moderate annuity, which she instantly and haughtily refused, positively declaring that she *never had made any confession of guilt;* that the whole was a scheme of his own vicious jealousy to get rid of her; and that she had only said, he might *just as well* suspect the Attorney-General, who had never said a civil thing to her, *as any body else.* She dared him to *prove* the least impropriety on her part; and yet he had cruelly turned her out of his house, and proclaimed his innocent wife to be a guilty woman. Mr. Cuffe saw she had been too many for him every way! he durst not give more publicity to the affair; and therefore agreed to allow her a very handsome annuity, whereon she lived a happy life, and died but a few years since."

Mr. Walsh exchanged from the Life-guards, in which Capt. Pellew held his commission. Prior to his quitting the regiment he had resided with his wife a good deal at the barracks in Hyde-Park, she being young and thoughtless, unhappily received with too much readiness, those attentions which military men, often think themselves at liberty to pay to every female. The consequence was such as might be expected to result from such infatuation. A close attachment was formed between Capt. Pellew and the lady; and at length in a fatal moment, she agreed to sacrifice her character, by eloping with the object of her blind affection. In about a month she went off with him, from her father's house, where she had been residing for some time during the absence of her husband.—They came to Paris, whither they were followed by Mr. Walsh, he prefering what is called the satisfaction of a gentleman, to pursuing any legal means of redress. A Mr. F. came over with him, and by him the meeting was arranged with Mr. H. on the part of Capt. Pellew. They were attended on the ground by Mr. K. as the friend of Mr. F., and by Capt. H. as the friend of Mr. H. Dr. T. was also present. The distance was twelve full paces, and they were to fire together by signal.—When it was given, the pistol of Mr. W. was immediately discharged. Capt. P. did not fire, and it is said, that he never intended to do so. Mr. W.'s ball passed through the right temple, into the brain of Capt. P. who expired even before his body reached the ground. Thus from the consequences of one false step, perished a gallant young officer, the pride of his regiment, the delight of his friends, and the darling and only child of his now distressed parents.

Lord Camelford had for some time been acquainted with a

Mrs. S—m—s, who had formerly been the mistress of Mr. Best, his lordship's intimate acquaintance. It having been represented to him, that Mr. Best had said something to this woman which was prejudicial to his lordship's character or feelings, he was so much incensed that meeting that gentleman on the 6th of March, at the Prince of Wales's coffee-house, he said in the presence of several persons, "I find, Sir, that you have spoken of me in the most unwarrantable terms." Mr. Best replied that he was quite unconscious of having done so. Lord Camelford said he was not ignorant of what he had reported to Mrs. S—m—s, and declared him to be a scoundrel, a liar, and a ruffian.

In the course of the evening Mr. Best transmitted to Lord Camelford the strongest assurances that the information which he had received was false, and stated that as his lordship had acted under a false impression, he would be satisfied by the retraction of the words which had been used. Lord Camelford refusing to give this reasonable satisfaction, Mr. Best left the coffee-house in considerable agitation, and a note being received soon after by Lord Camelford, the people of the house concluded it was a challenge, and gave information at the police-office, but no steps were taken until two o'clock in the morning, when persons were ineffectually placed at Lord Camelford's door. At his lordship's lodgings, in Bond-street, he inserted the following declaration in his will:—

"There are many other matters which at another time I might be induced to mention, but I will say nothing more at present than that in the present contest I am fully and entirely the aggressor, as well in the spirit, as in the letter of the word. Should I therefore lose my life in a contest of my own seeking, I most solemnly forbid any of my friends or relations, let them be of whatsoever description they may, from instituting any vexatious proceedings against my antagonist; and should, notwithstanding the above declaration on my part, the laws of the land be put in force against him, I desire that this part of my will may be made known to the king, in order that his royal heart may be moved to extend his mercy towards him."

After writing this declaration, he left his lodgings between one and two o'clock on Wednesday morning, March 9th, and slept at a tavern, probably with a view to escape the vigilance of the police. Agreeable to an arrangement between the seconds, his lordship and Mr. Best met early in the morning at a coffee-house in Oxford-street, and there Mr. Best renewed his endeavours to induce the retraction of the offensive expressions. "Camelford," said he, "we have been friends, and I know the unsuspecting generosity of your nature. Upon my honor you have been imposed upon by a strumpet. Do not insist on expressions under which one of us must fall." To this remonstrance Lord Camelford replied, "Best, this is child's play; the thing must go on." It is asserted, that notwithstanding his refusal of accommodation, he, upon mature reflection, acquitted Best of having said what Mrs. S—m—s attributed to that gentleman—that he confidently acknowledged to his second he was in error, and that Best was a man of honor, but that he could not prevail upon himself to retract words which he had once used.

The reason he rejected all accommodation was, he knew Best was reputed the first shot in England, and he erroneously conceived that his reputation might be injured by the slightest concession to such an adversary. He and Mr. Best rode to Kensington, and were followed by the seconds in a post-chaise. On their arrival at the Horse and Groom, about a quarter before eight, they dismounted, and walked to the fields at the rere of Holland-house, where they were placed at thirty paces distance, which, upon being measured, proved to be just twenty-nine yards. Lord Camelford fired first, but without effect. A space of several seconds intervened—during which, by the manner and attitude of Mr. Best, he appeared to several persons who viewed the duel at a distance, as if he were asking whether his lordship was satisfied. Mr. Best then fired, and his lordship instantly fell at full length. The two seconds and Mr. Best instantly ran to his assistance, when he seized the latter by the hand, and exclaimed, "Best, I am a dead man,—you have killed me, but I freely forgive you."

The report of the pistols having alarmed several persons who were at work near the spot; they hastened towards the place, which induced Mr. Best and his second to fly for safety. One of Lord Holland's gardeners called to his fellow-labourers to stop them. On the arrival of this man, Lord Camelford's second, who till then had been supporting him, ran for a surgeon; and Mr.

Thompson, of Kensington, soon after arrived to his assistance. His lordship asked the gardener why he ordered the gentlemen to be stopped—declared that he did not wish it, that he was himself the aggressor, that he forgave the gentleman who shot him, and that he hoped God would forgive him too. A chair having been obtained, he was carried into Little Holland House, the residency of Mr. Ottey. Messengers were sent for Mr. Knight, Mr. Home, and the Rev. Mr. Cockburne, who was his lordship's cousin. His clothes were cut off by the surgeons; they examined and pronounced the wound mortal. During the first day he suffered great agony, but he lingered without acute pain from Thursday till Saturday evening, when mortification put a period to his life.

To the Rev. Mr. Cockburne, who remained continually with him, he expressed his confidence in the goodness and mercy of God. In the moments of his severest agony, he cried out that he sincerely hoped the agonies he then endured might expiate the sins he had committed. "I wish," says Mr. Cockburne, who wrote a pamphlet on the subject, "with all my soul, that the unthinking votaries of dissipation and infidelity could all have been present at the death-bed of this poor man—could have heard his expressions of contrition for past misconduct, and of reliance upon the mercy of his Creator—could have heard his dying exhortation to one of his intimate friends, to live in future a life of peace and virtue, I think it would have made an impression on their minds, as it did on mine, not easily to be effaced."

Thus died Lord Camelford, in the prime of life, and at the age of twenty-nine. His imperfections and follies have frequently been the public topic; but he had some valuable qualities, and released many a debtor from the prisons of the metropolis. The verdict of the coroner's jury, was "wilful murder against some person or persons unknown." A bill of indictment was prefered against Mr. Best, but it was thrown out by the grand jury.

On opening the body after death, it appeared that the ball had penetrated the right breast, between the fourth and fifth ribs, breaking the latter, and making its way through the right lobe of the lungs into the sixth dorsal vertebræ, where it lodged, having completely divided the spinal marrow. In the chest there were upwards of six quarts of extravasated blood, which had compressed the lungs so as to prevent them in performing their functions. From the moment in which he was wounded, all the parts below the divided spinal marrow were motionless and insensible, and as he could not expectorate, the left lung became filled with mucus, which ultimately produced suffocation and death.

He bequeathed one thousand pounds to purchase a particular spot of ground, in the Canton of Berne, in Switzerland, situated between three trees, where he wished to be interred.

A certain police officer having attempted to prevent this duel, Camelford handed him three hundred guineas, desiring him at the same time to retire, or he would blow his brains out, and those who knew his lordship, think the officer was prudent in retiring with or without the money. It is alleged that Mr. Best and his second, as well as the second of Lord Camelford, fled at the approach of a stranger, leaving his lordship upon his back in a field covered with several inches of water, yet when he was expiring, he declared that all the parties had acted like men of honor.

The fatal duel between Dillon and Kyan was also about a female.

Messrs. Manuel and Beaumont were wealthy agents on the Parisian Change; Manuel had six children and a wife, with whom he lived on very happy terms. He received two anonymous intimations that she was habitually unfaithful to him, but he tore them with playfulness, and treated the accusation with contempt; a third however was received, naming the place of rendezvous, with the hour and signal which would procure him an admission. He went and gave the signal, and was admitted by his own wife, who embraced him as her seducer Beaumont. Manuel was a Pole; he sold out all his French possessions, and retired to his native country, offering his wife forgiveness if she would give up the seducer, and remain with her six children, which she declined. In about six months afterwards, having business to Paris, he met Beaumont on the Change, they had some words, and the duel ensued, in which Manuel received a ball through his heart from the seducer of his wife!

The sister of a naval officer, named Loyd, had been promised marriage, and seduced by a Capt. Powell—poor Loyd got leave of absence to attend the wedding, which was declined by the seducer, a duel was the consequence, in the county of Westmeath, and both were killed at the second fire. Before the death of Loyd, he eagerly enquired if his antagonist was dead, and being answered that he was shot dead through the brain, he took off a ring which he had promised to his sister, and sent it with a message, that he had avenged her wrongs.

The daughter of a widow lady, residing at Carcasone, was seduced in Nov. 1826, by a Capt. of Chasseurs, garrisoned in that city. The consequence soon became apparent, and the captain was urged in vain to marry the young lady. He departed with his regiment to Hesden. The young lady, accompanied by her mother and brother, followed him, and pressed him again on the subject; but he refused, alleging that he was not rich enough. The brother offered to give a portion of his fortune to his sister, but the captain still refused. The young lady driven to despair, resolved on dying, and repairing to the cemetery fell down motionless. The brother sent a challenge to the captain, and after four shots on each side were fired, at twenty-five paces ineffectually, the fifth entered the seducer's eye, fractured his skull, and killed him on the spot.

Messrs. Barnard and Elphinstone, two intimate friends and relatives, fought about a lady on Crawley Common, in the July of 1825, when Mr. E. was wounded in the side by the second shot.

A meeting took place in April, 1823, between Lieutenant Colonel Ch——rch——ll, late of the Grenadier Guards, and Lieutenant F——, of the 13th Light Dragoons. The latter received the fire of his antagonist, but did not return it. The cause of quarrel was supposed to be of a domestic nature.

A Mrs. Massey and her daughter came from St. Domingo to New Orleans. Miss M. had married a Mr. Anthony, who suddenly absconded, and went to the Wood of Natches. She was divorced from this unnatural husband, which induced an imprudent person to offend her at a ball; her brother challenged the aggressor; and the meeting led to four other duels, of which two were fatal.

A very fine and amiable girl who, unfortunately for her family, is now no more, having been offended by the inconsiderate behaviour of a young gentleman to whom she was unknown, mentioned her case in confidence to her step-father, observing that she was governed in so doing by a conviction that his discretion would prevent a repetition of the insult. A letter, of which the following is a copy, was immediately left with the family of General K——, where the offending gentleman occasionally called:—

> "Sir,—One of those young ladies who for nearly fourteen years has called me father, has prefered a complaint against you for an insult which she received in this avenue. Although she has an uncle, a brother, and several cousins who are naval or military officers, and although two of them dined yesterday at this cottage, she reserved for my ear the complaint of your misconduct. I request in the course of this day a written apology, the publication of which may prevent a repetition of such behaviour towards any respectable female in my neighbourhood. My respect for Mrs. General K. and the remainder of that estimable family, who have hitherto given you credit for the behaviour of a gentleman, has prevented the adoption of other measures, which might render your appearance in Trinity College, or in this avenue, peculiarly unpleasant to yourself."

In a very short time after the delivery of this letter, the individual to whom it was addressed, accompanied by Mr. H. K. called and delivered an unsealed letter, which was so very creditable to the writer, that its publication would have been ungenerous; and we understand that the young gentleman who wrote it, has since become a useful lecturer on Christian morals.

In the spring of 1829, a Major G. having frequently intruded himself on the attention of a young lady, who resides near Dublin, while her father was absent upon business in England, and her brother was with his regiment in India, she very properly communicated all the circumstances to her mother, who requested to speak with the officer, and the result was such as might be naturally looked for—relatives were named, and we were amongst the nearest, who would protect the lady against unauthorized intrusions. His card was tendered with an apology for the past, and a pledge upon his honor that he would intrude no more. Towards the family of the two last named young ladies, (for they were step-sisters) we speak advisedly when we assert that it is not very safe to be offenders.

Captain Kepple has recorded a Persian criticism upon duelling, which is particularly applicable to cases arising out of aggressions upon female feelings, character, or honor. "How foolish it is for a man who wishes to kill his enemy, to expose his own life when he can accomplish his purpose with so much greater safety by shooting him from behind a rock." It was for an insult offered to the wife of Hamilton, by ejecting her from her lands and castle in the night, that her indignant husband shot the Regent Murray from a window.

A Captain Fitzgerald having grievously offended against the honor of the Kingston family, and exchanged four shots with the present Viscount Lorton, attempted a renewal of the trespass near Mitchelstown, in Ireland, and was shot in his bed-chamber by the late Earl, who would not allow his son to hazard his life again in single combat. Here was a very strong case indeed. The Earl of Kingston was tried and honorably acquitted by his peers, there being no witnesses to prove the case as we have stated it. But let us now suppose, what is within the range of possibility, merely as an admonition for a class of ruffians, who, like the Duke of Buckingham, would wrong a husband, or a father, and then slay him in a single combat. The sister, wife, or daughter of Virginius is seduced, and he slays the aggressor in a gust of passion, saying—the laws have not provided unction for my wounds. If I shot ten thieves for the midnight plunder of my orchard, I should not be imprisoned for a single hour. I know that I shall now be executed like a felon for the killing of this villain, who has plundered me of more than all the orchards in the universe could purchase; and I have prefered such death to being slain by the seducer, who might have possibly survived me in a single combat. I will now make an offering of my life upon the scaffold of my country, in order to force a lazy legislation, by a reflection on my sorrows, to raise a better fence round the domestic circle. I shall at least have left one terrible example to deter all future libertines. We are far from defending the horrible crime of assassination; but we contend for it, that if a father, a husband, or a brother, were to avenge a gross aggression upon female honor, although he should become a victim to the laws, he would have more of reason on his side, than if he were to give the aggressor such a meeting as poor Loyd unfortunately gave to Capt. Powell. If men must fight there ought to be something of equality between them.

"If" (says a celebrated writer), "having seized a man who has murdered my wife, I should carry him before a tribunal, and demand justice, what should we think of that judge, if he should order that the criminal and I should cast lots which of us should be hanged."

As we remember several cases in which the too captious spirit of a lady, has led an estimable gentleman into a fatal duel, we shall close this article, referring them to page 31 of the Court of Honor, and by reminding them, that the idea of a lady has ever been associable with tenderness and grace, and that chivalry reminded her of the natural softness and humanity of her character, when prescribing any service for a knight. Schiller makes De Lorges, the knight, drop down into a horrible pit, to take a gauntlet from the midst of the wild beasts, but it was only that he might toss it to the lady Kunigund, and then turn from her for ever. The knight, in the Mort d' Arthur, will be found performing another dangerous service, but the woman at whose mandate he performed it, for ever after lost her valiant knight. "If a woman obliged me to perform it," (says an aged officer in a famous romance) "I would perform it, but never see her more."

> "Gentle maid should never ask,
> Of knighthood vain or bloody task,
> And beauty's eyes should ever be,
> Like the twin stars that soothe the sea,
> And beauty's breath should whisper peace,
> And bid the storm of battle cease."

In future, should any virtuous female, either married or single, be placed in embarrassing circumstances, by the unlicensed assiduities of a ruffian, we request, that after furnishing him with an extract from this page, she may, if necessary, have a confidential statement of the facts left with us, for the writer of the letter in page 123, she may rely upon its falling into the hands of one who honors female worth, and can render an efficient service, without hazarding the life of husband, brother, father, friend, or lover.

INFLUENCE OF WOMAN

We have asserted in our "School for Patriots," that "women have frequently become the rivals of men in deeds of patriotism, and the influence which they possess so justly in society, is convertible into a lever of the first importance, for the elevation of a nation's moral and political character.

"Mrs. Hannah More, a writer of considerable celebrity, has declared that among the talents, for the application of which, women are peculiarly accountable, there is one, the importance of which they cannot rate too highly, and that is influence, for the general state of civilized society has a considerable dependance upon their prevailing habits and opinions.

"The seeds of virtue and vice are generally deposited in the infant heart by the mother, the nurse, or the female attendants; and when their fruits are knitting at the approach to manhood, they may be blighted or mellowed by the female glance; for men are well aware that their reputation is promoted by the favourable opinion of the other sex, and at every stage of life we may easily discover that the opinion of a virtuous female commands, at least, a respectful consideration.

"As the extension and direction of this influence for the promotion of moral, religious and patriotic objects, appears to us of the very first importance, we shall hastily throw together a few remarks upon the subject, reserving for a future effort the gratifying task of placing the character of women in the point of view it merits.

"Although women have generally been the victims of injustice, yet in some parts of the world they have received the homage which was their due. The arts have frequently been called in as auxiliaries in the celebration of their virtues, and

126

authors of the first respectability have done ample justice to their merits.

"Plutarch mentions an instance in which the women of a besieged city made its warriors blush, because of its dishonorable surrender; and others who seeing their relations fly before the enemy, secured the city gates, and compelled the recreants to return in search of death, or victory. During a civil war in Gaul, the women, having thrown themselves between contending armies, and effected a reconciliation, were afterwards honored by admission to the public deliberations, and appointed arbitrators between the neighbouring States.

"During one of the Punic wars, the Carthaginian ladies cut off their hair to make bow strings for the archers. At Rome the husband received the honor for his wounds in the estimation of his wife, at whose feet he deposited the spoils which he had taken from the enemy. In a single day Hortensia gave an example of eloquence to her own sex, courage to the men, and humanity to tyrants.

"Among the Jews we find Judith successfully reproving the desponding chieftains of Bethulia. A mother encouraging the last of her tortured children to be faithful unto death, and a group of pious women surrounding a Saviour's cross, when every man, except the beloved disciple, had deserted.

"In all ages and countries the women have been more zealous than the men, in making proselytes to their religious tenets. At communion we generally observe four women for one of the other sex. Women first carried the Christian religion successfully to thrones, making their very charms subservient to the extension of the gospel. This was particularly the case in France, England, Germany, Bavaria, Hungary, Bohemia, Lithuania, Poland, Prussia, and other places.

"In the fourth century, St. Jerome was the zealous panegyrist of the female sex. His very style was softened and conformable to the gentleness of his subject when he treated of Marcella, Paulina, Eustochium, and other Roman ladies, who had embraced the greatest austerities of the Christian religion, and diligently applied themselves to the study of the Hebrew language, that they might the better understand the writings of the Jewish legislator.

"Mrs. More expresses an anxious hope, that in a country where her sex enjoys the advantage of a liberal education, reasonable legislation, pure religion, and all the endearing satisfactions of equal, virtuous, and social intercourse, women will not content themselves with polishing, when they are armed with the powers to reform man; with captivating for a day, when they may be successfully labouring for eternity. She has endeavoured to excite in them a spirit of generous enterprise for the correction of the public morals, and fanning the religious flame which has latterly become so languid. She forcibly dwells upon the important advantages resulting from the united exertion of beauty, virtue, rank, and talents, in the indulgence of a patriotism which is at once both firm, and perfectly consistent with all the natural delicacy of her sex.

"In order to secure the success of such a noble undertaking, it is necessary that women should reflect upon their powers, and endeavour to extend them daily. They should chase from their society the professed duellist, seducer, drunkard, gambler and blasphemer;—they should promote the reformation of the stage, and the reclamation of their abused and fallen sisterhood."

"Every lady who holds a respectable situation in society, may stretch out a saving hand to a fallen woman, without compromising her own dignity."

QUARRELS ABOUT RELIGION

"Their mouths full of the pious praises of the living God, and their
hands stained with the blood of his most favoured creatures."

Will it be believed, that men professing to be zealous for a
peaceful Gospel, should slay each other in a quarrel about
creeds.

In July, 1791, Mr. Graham, a special pleader, and Mr. Julius, an
attorney, fought at Blackheath, near London, having had a quarrel about their faith. Mr. Graham was shot through the femoral
artery and killed—the parties were most intimate friends, and
fought under the coersion of what they thought public opinion.

In 1802, Mr. Bernard Coile, of the Linen Hall, in Dublin,
fought the Rt. Hon. Mr. Ogle, a privy counsellor, when eight shots
were fired, in a religious and electioneering quarrel. Mr. Coile,
and his second, the facetious Counsellor Lysught, dined with us
immediately after the duel, of which we shall give all the particulars under the electioneering head.

In Dec. 1826, a meeting took place at the rere of the barracks
in Cork, between Lt. Redmond Byrne, on the half pay of the 15th
regiment, and Lt. Martin Sullivan, on the half pay of the 19th regiment, the former attended by Mr. —— Underwood, and the latter by Mr. Wm. Raynes—after an exchange of two shots each, the
seconds interfered, and the business was adjusted. It had its origin in some reflections thrown out by Lt. S. on the Roman
Catholic clergy, which were repelled by Lt. B. in the strongest
negative that the English language could admit of.

We could mention several duels which have arisen out of similar disputes, but we trust the time is not far distant when men
shall cease to

"Hate each other for the love of God."

APPEALS TO THE LAWS

"A suit of armour you may chuse,
I chuse a suit at law."

Mr. Curran was a gentleman of unquestionable courage, as had been proved upon several occasions, yet when he was publicly and wantonly assaulted with a whip, he very properly appealed to the bench for the correction of that violence which was at war with all the decencies of civilized society.

Mr. Phillips, the barrister, who was born in a country where the Point of Honor is well understood, and who, in more instances than one, has shewn he is not too passive under insult, was engaged in April, 1824, in a prosecution for an assault, on Edward Harvey Foster, an officer, and addressing the jury he said, the "prisoner perhaps conceives, that being found guilty of horsewhipping a man in the street is a triumph; but it was an act of a vile, miscreant, and could not stain, in the smallest degree, the character of the gallant officer. The laws of honor are a code of laws for equals, and not for a man who spurns them in the first instance and then claims the benefit of them." He concluded by saying, he trusted the jury would send the prosecutor home with an unspotted character. The prisoner was found guilty, and in passing sentence, the chairman of the Westminster sessions said, "The prosecutor had pursued the best and most honorable course, he had been violently assaulted, and in order to send him to his regiment with honor, and to mark the sense of the court the sentence was, that the defendant be imprisoned three months."

All the summer assizes in Tyrone, Mr. John Irvine was sentenced to eighteen months imprisonment, and to find surety for two thousand pound to keep the peace, for assaulting Mr. Alexander Sinclair and challenging him to fight a duel. Mr. C. S. Monk was sentenced to eight months imprisonment for delivering the message.

In the case of Hume Blacker against the Rev. Joseph Shepherd, Mr. Blacker swore that Shepherd desired him to take his ground, at the same time making use of these expressions, "with this single barrelled gun of mine," alluding to a fowling piece which he held in his hand, "I will fight you with your double barrel," and then cocked his gun. For those expressions he was punished.

The following extract from a Dublin newspaper, is inserted to show with what facility, a gentleman can obtain redress for any provoking or insulting language.

Court of King's Bench—SMITH *a* BROWNING.—Mr. Driscol made application on the part of the plaintiff, for a criminal information against the defendant, for using language to him calculated to provoke him to fight a duel. The expression particularly complained of was, that "he," the plaintiff, "was a rascal."

The Chief Justice. You need not go further. Take a conditional rule.

Captain G——, of one of the regiments of Footguards, applied to Mr. Dyer, the presiding magistrate at Marlborough-street Office, in London, for a warrant against Captain ——, of the Light Dragoons.

He stated, that he had been informed, with a considerable degree of surprise, that Captain —— had expressed a determination to shoot him wherever he could meet with him, and that he carried a loaded pistol about him for that purpose. He was much surprised, he said, at being told this, as he had no acquaintance with the Captain, did not even know his person, and the cause of his displeasure he understood, had relation to a female. This morning the Captain G. had occasion to call on Lord Spencer Churchill, at his house in Margaret-street, Cavendish-square, and while in the act of knocking at the door, a person, answering the description he got of Captain ——, came up to him, and in a confused manner asked him if he was not Captain G. at the same time putting his hand up to his breast, as if to draw something from it; fortunately he, Captain G. had presence of mind enough to answer in the negative. The solicitor of Captain G., who accompanied him with other friends to this office, stated to Mr. Dyer that the reason which induced Captain G. to take this course rather than resort to the usual mode upon such occasions was, that he, Captain G., had been unfortunately engaged in a duel in which he shot his antagonist dead, and that his (Captain G.'s) friends were in consequence committed in recognizances to a large amount that he should keep the peace.

Mr. Dyer immediately granted the warrant, and ordered the officer Plank to proceed forthwith in the execution of it. Plank lost no time in doing so, and after some enquiry discovered that Captain —— was in custody of Thoroughgood, the sheriff's officer, for debt, who on Plank's expressing a wish to be satisfied that such was the fact, produced the writ, which of course put an end to Plank's commission; Captain G. however said, that he had every reason to expect that he should be liberated that evening, and that on Monday he would attend at the office. He was liberated according to his expectation, but immediately left town to join his regiment, which is on foreign service. Between four and five o'clock on Sunday morning, Captain G., accompanied by a friend of his, drove up to Plank's house in a chaise, and requested him to proceed with them to Portsmouth, where they said they learned Captain —— had gone. Plank, however, having more urgent business on his hands in town, declined to do so, but gave the warrant to Captain G.'s friend, and they departed with the intention of proceeding to that port immediately.

Writing as we are for the Christian moralist who scruples fighting, and for the point of honor-man, who would abide by public opinion, we think it is our duty, under various heads, to furnish useful hints for every class of readers.

RECOGNIZANCE TO KEEP THE PEACE

"Provide such surety as you will not forfeit."

As an erroneous opinion is too prevalent respecting the nature of recognizances, we acquaint our readers that Judge Burton having learned an affair of honor was in contemplation, had the parties, Lord Bingham and Mr. James Browne, brought before him, at Castle-bar, and bound them and sureties in recognizances to the amount of nine or ten thousand pounds on each side to keep the peace. His Lordship warned them that if they went to France, and had a meeting there, they and their bail would forfeit the recognizances.

Upon this subject Hone has the following passage in his Every Day Book, vol 2. p 945.

"Whereas certain persons, who contemn the laws of religion, are nevertheless mindful of the law of the land: and whereas it is supposed by some of such persons, that parties contemplating to fight a duel, and bound over to keep the peace, may, notwithstanding, fight such duel in foreign parts: be it known that the law which extends protection to all its subjects, can also punish them for breach of duty, and that therefore offences by duelling beyond sea, are indictable and punishable in manner and form, the same as if such duels were fought within the United Kingdom."

We cannot close this article without remarking, that it is strange the duellist should hazard life, which frequently involves the interests of his most intimate connexions; while he is frequently restrained from fighting to preserve a trifling penalty. This speaks a volume.

GAMBLING QUARRELS

"I've set my life upon the cast."

Some of the most desperate duels have arisen out of gambling and racing quarrels. The case of Major Oneby which we shall hereafter give at length was one of this description. A Mr. Gorman shot an officer on the North Strand, near Dublin, in consequence of a difference at play. And in 1824 a Mr. Westall shot Capt. Gourlay at Edinburgh, in a gambling quarrel, which was thus described by a correspondent in the British Traveller:—

"Mr. Westall, who shot Capt. Gourlay in the late duel, had formerly travelled for Messrs. James Fisher and Co., a London House of the first eminence in the lace trade. At the late Doncaster races he lost a bet of seventy guineas to Capt. Gourlay, who also lost a bet at the same time to a friend of Mr. Westalls. On Saturday last, Capt. Gourlay and Mr. Westall met at the Bull Inn, in this city, recognising each other with mutual civility and apparent friendship. After some conversation the Captain reminded Mr. Westall of his bet, which that gentleman acknowledged, but added, that he was authorised by his friend, to set off the bet which he had won from Capt. Gourlay, against that which he (Mr. Westall) had lost. An altercation ensuing, the Captain applied the term swindler to Mr. Westall, who, in return, called the Captain a liar. On this the Captain snatching up the poker, made a blow at Mr. Westall's head, which it missed, but descending on his shoulder, the poker snapt in two by the force of the blow, which for some minutes rendered him insensible. On recovering, Mr. Westall went into the Coffee-room, where after much warm language, a meeting was appointed for the following morning, at Salisbury Craggs. Capt. G. accompanied by his second, Capt. D., and a surgeon, at the time and place appointed, met Mr. W., who was, however, unaccompanied by a second; Mr. J. who had engaged to act as such, being detained by his father, who had some suspicion of the intended meeting, and was labouring under severe indisposition. Under this disappointment, the duel was suspended, and the parties mutually agreed to adjourn the meeting to Queen's-Ferry, that Mr. Westall, in the interval, might provide himself with another second. The parties met together at South Ferry, Capt. Gourlay, Capt. D., with the surgeon, and Mr. Westall, with his second, Mr. D—s. They all crossed together in a boat, and proceeded to an eminence, where, preliminaries being adjusted, the parties took their stations, and Capt. Gourlay receiving Mr. Westall's ball, fell dead upon the spot."

Innumerable cases might be furnished for this class; which, the impartial reader must admit, has very trifling intimacy with the point of honor.

We hope that in future men who value honorable feeling, will avoid the sending or accepting of a challenge on the subject of disputed property, or wagers.

OBSOLETE REGULATIONS

"This is a very pretty quarrel as it stands."

The absurdity of the Irish Fire-eaters' opinions on the point of honor, will appear conspicuous upon a perusal of those rules which have been adopted in Dublin, Galway, Tipperary, and other places, and which seem to claim insertion in this volume.

Sir Jonah Barrington says, "So many quarrels arose without sufficiently *dignified* provocation, and so many things were considered as quarrels *of course*, which were not quarrels at all, that the principal fire-eaters' of the South, saw clearly that disrepute was likely to be thrown, both on the science and its professors, and thought it full time to interfere and arrange matters upon a proper, steady, rational, and moderate footing, and to regulate the time, place, and other circumstances of duelling, so as to govern all Ireland on one principle, thus establishing a uniform national code of the *lex pugnandi*, proving, as Hugo Grotius did, that it was for the benefit of all belligerents, to adopt the same code and regulations.

"In furtherance of this object a branch society had been formed in Dublin, the 'Knights of Tara,' which met once a month at the theatre in Capel-street; gave premiums for fencing; and proceeded in the most laudably systematic manner. The amount of the admission money was laid out in silver cups, and given to the best fencers as prizes, at quarterly exhibitions of the pupils and amateurs.

"The theatre of the Knights of Tara, on those occasions was always overflowing, the combatants were dressed in close cambric jackets garnished with ribbons, each wearing the favourite colour of his fair one, bunches of ribbon also dangled at their knees, and roses ornamented their morocco slippers, which had buff soles to prevent noise in their lounges.

"No masks or visors were used, on the contrary, every feature was uncovered and its inflections all visible. The ladies appeared in full morning dresses, each handing his foil to her champion for the day, and their presence animating the singular exhibition. From the stage boxes likewise the prizes were handed to the conquerors by the fair ones, accompanied each with a wreath of laurel, and a smile, then more valued than a hundred victories! The tips of the foils were blackened, and therefore instantly betrayed the hits on the cambric jacket, and proclaimed without doubt the successful combatant. All was decorum, gallantry, spirit and good temper.

"The Knights of Tara had also a select committee to decide on all actual questions of honor referred to them; to reconcile differences, if possible; if not, to adjust the terms and continuance of single combat.—Doubtful points were solved generally on the peaceable side, provided no women were insulted or defamed; but when that was the case, the knights were inexorable, and blood must be seen. They were constituted by ballot, something in the manner of the Jockey Club, but without the possibility of being dishonorable, or the opportunity of cheating each other.

"This most agreeable and useful association did not last above two or three years. I cannot tell why it broke up. I rather think, however, the original fire-eaters thought it frivolous, or did not like their own ascendency to be rivalled. It was said, that they threatened direct hostility against the knights; and I am the more disposed to believe this, because, soon after, a comprehensive code of the laws and points of honor was issued from the southern fire-eaters, with directions that it should be strictly observed by all gentlemen throughout the kingdom, and kept in their pistol cases, that ignorance might never be pleaded. This code was not circulated in print, but very numerous written copies were sent to the different country clubs, &c. My father got one for his sons, and I transcribed most (I believe not all) of it into some blank leaves. These rules brought the whole business of duelling into a focus, and have been acted upon down to the present day. They called them in Galway the Thirty-six Commandments.

"As far as my copy went, they appear to run as follows:—

"The Practice of Duelling and the Point of Honor, settled at Clonmel summer assizes, 1777, by the gentlemen delegates of Tipperary, Galway, Mayo, Sligo, and Roscommon, and prescribed for general adoption throughout Ireland.

RULE I.

"The first offence requires the first apology, though the retort may have been more offensive than the insult. Example—A tells B he is impertinent, &c. B retorts that he lies: yet A must make the first apology, because he gave the first offence; and then, after one fire, B may explain away the retort by a subsequent apology.

RULE II.

"But if the parties would rather fight on, then after two shots each, (but in no case before) B. may explain first, and A. apologise afterwards.

"N. B. The above rules apply to all cases of offences in retort, not of a stronger class than the example.

RULE III.

"If a doubt exist who gave the first offence, the decision rests with the seconds. If they won't decide or can't agree, the matter must proceed to two shots, or to a hit, if the challenger require it.

RULE IV.

"When the *lie direct* is the first offence, the aggressor must either beg pardon in express terms, exchange two shots previous to apology, or three shots followed up by explanation; or fire on till a severe hit be received by one party or the other.

RULE V.

"As a blow is strictly prohibited, in ordinary circumstances amongst gentlemen, no verbal apology can be received for such an insult; the alternatives therefore are, the offender handing a cane to the injured party, to be used on his own back, at the same time begging pardon; firing on until one or both are disabled; or exchanging three shots and then asking pardon, *without* the cane.

"If swords are used, the parties engage until one is well blooded, disabled, or disarmed; or until after receiving a wound, and blood being drawn the aggressor begs pardon.

"N.B. A *disarm* is considered the same as a *disable:* the *disarmer* may (strictly) break his adversary's sword; but if it be the challenger who is disarmed, it is considered ungenerous to do so.

In case the challenged be disarmed, and refuses to ask pardon or atone, he must not be *killed,* as formerly; but the challenger may lay his own sword on the aggressors shoulder, then break the aggressor's sword, and say 'I spare your life,' the challenged can never revive that quarrel the challenger may.

RULE VI.

"If A gives B the lie, and B retorts by a blow, (being the two greatest offences,) no reconciliation *can* take place until after two discharges each, or a severe hit; *after* which B may beg A's pardon humbly for the blow, and then A may explain simply for the lie; because a blow is *never* allowable, and the offence of the lie therefore merges in it. (See preceding rule.)

"N.B. Challenges for undivulged causes may be reconciled on the ground, after one shot. An explanation on the slightest hit should be sufficient in such cases, because no personal offence transpired.

RULE VII.

"But no apology can be received, in any case, after the parties have actually taken their ground, without exchange of fires.

RULE VIII.

"In the above case, no challenger is obliged to divulge his cause of challenge, (if private) unless required by the challenged so to do *before* their meeting.

RULE IX.

"All imputations of cheating at play, races, &c. to be considered equivalent to a blow; but may be reconciled after one shot, on admitting their falsehood, and begging pardon publicly.

RULE X.

"Any insult to a lady, under a gentleman's care or protection, to be considered as by one degree a greater offence than if given to the gentleman personally, and to be regulated accordingly.

RULE XI.

"Offences originating or accruing from the support of a lady's reputation, to be considered as less unjustifiable than any others of the same class, and as admitting of slighter apologies by the aggressor. This is to be considered by the circumstances of the case, but *always* favorable to the lady.

RULE XII.

"In simple, unpremeditated rencontres with the small sword, or couteau-de-chasse, the rule is, first draw, first sheath; unless blood be drawn: then both sheath, and proceed to investigation.

RULE XIII.

"No dumb shooting, or firing in the air, admissible *in any case*. The challenger ought not to have challenged without receiving offence; and the challenged ought, if he gave offence, to have made an apology before he came on the ground: therefore *children's play* must be dishonorable on one side or the other, and is accordingly prohibited.

RULE XIV.

"Seconds to be of equal rank in society with the principals whom they attend; inasmuch as a second may either choose or chance to become a principal, and equality is indispensible.

RULE XV.

"Challenges are never to be delivered at night, unless the party to be challenged intends leaving the place before morning, for it is desirable to avoid all hot-headed proceedings.

RULE XVI.

"The challenged has a right to choose his own weapon, unless the challenger gives his honor he is no swordsman; after which, however, he cannot decline any *second* species of weapon, proposed by the challenged.

RULE XVII.

"The challenged chooses his ground; the challenger his distance, the seconds fix the time and terms of firing.

RULE XVIII.

"The seconds load in presence of each other, unless they give their mutual honors that they have charged smooth and single, which should be held sufficient.

RULE XIX.

"Firing may be regulated—first, by signal; secondly, by word of command, or thirdly, at pleasure as may be agreeable to the parties. In the latter case, the parties may fire at their reasonable leisure, but *second presents* and *rests,* are strictly prohibited.

RULE XX.

"In all cases a miss-fire is equivalent to a shot, and a *snap,* or a *non-cock,* is to be considered as a miss-fire.

RULE XXI.

"Seconds are bound to attempt a reconciliation *before* the meeting takes place, or *after* sufficient firing, or hits, as specified.

RULE XXII.

"Any wound sufficient to agitate the nerves, and necessarily make the hand shake, must end the business for that day.

RULE XXIII.

"If the cause of meeting be of such a nature, that no apology can or will be received, the challenged takes his ground, and calls on the challenger to proceed as he chooses; in such cases firing at pleasure is the usual practise, but may be varied by agreement.

RULE XXIV.

"In slight cases, the second hands his principal but one pistol; but in gross cases, two, holding another case ready charged in reserve.

RULE XXV.

"Where seconds disagree and resolve to exchange shots themselves, it must be at the same time, and at right angles with their principals, thus:—

$$S$$
$$\cdot$$
$$\cdot$$
$$\cdot$$
$$\cdot$$
$$P \ldots\ldots\ldots\ldots\ldots P$$
$$\cdot$$
$$\cdot$$
$$\cdot$$
$$S$$

If with swords, side by side, with five paces interval.

"N. B. All matters and doubts not herein mentioned, will be explained and cleared up, by application to the committee who meet alternately at Clonmel and Galway, at the quarter sessions for that purpose.

"CROW RYAN,   President.
"JAMES KEOUGH," } Secretaries."
"AMBY BODKIN,

ADDITIONAL GALWAY RULES.

RULE I.

"No party can be allowed to bend his knee, or cover his side with his left hand; but may present at any level from the hip to the eye.

RULE II.

"None can either advance or retreat, if the ground be measured. If no ground be measured, either party may advance at his pleasure, even to touch muzzle; but neither can advance on his adversary after the fire, unless the adversary steps forward on him.

"N. B. The seconds on both sides, stand responsible for this last rule being *strictly* observed; bad cases having occurred from neglecting of it."

Perhaps we should apologise for copying so many pages from Sir Jonah Barrington, who is generally considered an apocryphal authority. To many of his readers the compilation of his "medley" may appear rather singular,—indeed the learned knight himself assures us that he thought the same, and had "got nearly half way through it, before he could account for the thing." In the preface he compliments some works of pure imagination, and the invention of matters of fact, for the attaining of extensive circulation, and its attending profits. We shall feel much obliged by his publishing a letter which he had from Edward Cook, and on which we shall have some remarks to offer in the School for Patriots.

THE IRISH DUELLIST

"Comes out, meets his friend, and for love knocks him down."

There is no part of the world, in which duelling has been productive of such serious evil as in the Emerald Isle. It was formerly practised there, to a most extravagant extent, and even yet there is scarcely a single hour elapses without a hostile meeting in some part of the island, although comparatively few of the cases are recorded in the public journals. There is not, we are convinced, a respectable family throughout that portion of the empire, which cannot tell of numerous wounds acquired in single combat. Love, law, electioneering, religion, politics, and numerous other most prolific sources of dispute, furnish fire-devourers with fair opportunities of becoming practically acquainted with all the forms of fighting.

Every family, which had the least pretensions to gentility, was sure to have those instruments most used in single combat. Sir Jonah says, "our family pistols, denominated pelters, were brass, the barrels were very long, and point blankers; they were included in the armoury of our ancient castle of Ballynakil, in the reign of Elizabeth, and had descended from father to son from that period. One of them was named Sweet-lips, the other the Darling. The family rapier was called Skiver the Pullet, by my grand-uncle, Captain Wheeler Barrington, who had fought with it repeatedly, and run through different parts of their persons, several Scotch officers who had challenged him all at once, for some national reflection. It was a very long and narrow bladed, straight cut-and-thrust, as sharp as a razor, with a silver hilt, and a guard of buff leather inside it.

"Our elections," says this author, "were more prolific in duels than any other public meetings: they very seldom originated at a horse race, a cock-fight, hunt, or at any place of amusement: folks then had pleasure in view, and 'something else to do' than to quarrel, but at all elections, or at assizes, or in fact at any place of business, almost every man, without any very particular or assignable reason, immediately became a violent partizan; and frequently a furious enemy to somebody else; and gentlemen often got themselves shot before they could tell what they were fighting about."

Mr. Lyttleton declared, in the House of Commons, on the 26th of April, 1825, amidst great cheers and laughter, that "the candidate who would dare to canvass leaseholders in Ireland, must be prepared to answer for his conduct at the pistol's mouth, and that the only unsettled point upon this subject in the Irish Courts of Honor was, whether indeed such an offending candidate was not bound to receive his adversaries fire without returning it." Such indeed was the melancholy fact until the contested elections of 1826, when the forty shilling freeholder forgot the landlord in the indulgence of his patriotism, a crime for which he has been since disfranchised. Mr. Colclough was shot by his own friend, Mr. Alcock, for allowing the committee of the former to canvass some freeholders, whose landlady had promised that they should "support the latter."

The following anecdote, which we copy from "the Clubs of London," is highly illustrative of electioneering dangers:—

"In the year 1790, the representation of the County of Down, was strongly contested between the eldest son of the then Lord Hillsborough, and the late Lord Castlereagh; amongst the lawyers engaged for the occasion, was Mr. W. Downes, after-wards Chief Justice of the Court of King's Bench. Previously to his setting out for Downpatrick, Mr. Downes happened to meet Curran, to whom he mentioned that he was retained for one of the parties; and added, that he was sorry to understand that much ill-will was expected to display itself—insomuch, that it was not unlikely but that the partizans of the candidates would proceed to duelling and bloodshed. 'For my part,' continued he, 'I shall keep clear of every subject but what is connected with my professional duties.' 'No doubt,' said Curran, 'you are perfectly well prepared.' 'Oh yes,' replied Downes, 'I have made myself master of all the *election cases.*' 'Very good,' replied Curran, 'yet however desirous you may be of keeping yourself clear of controversy and quarrels, some irritable bully may run foul of you; therefore I would recommend that you should have *Wogden's Case,* at your *fingers' ends.* 'Wogden's case!' observed Downes with surprise, 'I never heard of that case before! I am much obliged to you my dear fellow, for mentioning it; where shall I find the report of it?' 'I am surprised,' returned Curran, 'that you, so conversant with elections, should never have heard the *report* of Wogden's case. There are twenty shops in town where you can procure the case itself.' Mr. Downes, pleased with the hint, deferred his journey towards the theatre of war for that day, the whole of which he employed in ransacking every bookseller's shop in Dublin. At length he mentioned his difficulty to a brother barrister whom he met; and was not a little confounded when the latter, readily taking the joke, burst into a loud laugh at his simplicity, and told him, instead of continuing his researches among the booksellers, to step across the street to a *gun smith's shop,* where he would find the case in a minute." Wogden was a celebrated pistol maker.

The gallantry of the Irishman has frequently attempted to redeem the reputation of the duellist. In all affairs where women were concerned, the Irish point of honor-man became a most uncompromising champion. Barrington assets that "If any gentleman presumed to pass between a lady and the wall, in walking the streets of Dublin, he was considered as offering a personal affront to her escort, and if the parties wore swords, as was then customary, it is probable the first salutation to the offender would be, 'Draw Sir.' However, such offences usually ended in an apology to the lady for inadvertence. But if a man ventured into the boxes of the theatre, in his surtout or boots, or with his hat on, it was regarded as a general insult to every lady present, and he had little chance of escaping without a shot, or a thrust, before the following night."

We could mention several cases like the following, in which neglect of etiquette towards ladies has led to loss of life.

Where Talbot-street now stands, was once Marlborough-green, a sort of tea-drinking place, with singers, a band of music, &c. and was greatly frequented. One evening a young nobleman was descending the steps which led to the long room, and a gentleman with a party of ladies was going up, the latter in full dress, the former in boots and spurs; "D—n your boots," said the companion of the ladies, and proceeded with his party to the rooms. He had not sat with his party two minutes, when Lord —— hastily entered, and struck him across the shoulders with his rattan, saying, "follow me, Sir." Mr. —— started up; they both rushed down the steps, which were outside the room, upon the green, where a number of persons were walking and conversing. Lord —— drew a small sword, Mr. —— drew his. In a pass or two, Lord —— was run through the body, and lived but a few hours afterwards.

The English ambassador, when introducing George Robert Fitzgerald at the Court of France, represented that conspicuous Irishman as having fought no less than thirty duels, which induced the king to say, that his life would make an excellent appendix to that of Monsieur Jack, the Giant Killer. Having wronged the memory of Mr. Barrington in the introduction to this work, by saying twenty six, instead of thirty, we lose as little time as possible in making the *amende honorable.* We believe that out of the thirty duels, only six and twenty were fatal.

The individuals who composed the celebrated Hell-fire Club, were obliged to qualify themselves for that very honorable community, by the murder of at least one man in single combat. This rule was not quite so liberal as was that of the Gendarmes in France, who admitted persons, upon their swearing to fight at least one duel within the year ensuing.

Barrington says, "There was in 1782, a volunteer corps, which was called the 'Independent Light Horse.' They were not confined to one district, and none could be admitted but the younger brothers of the most respectable families. They were all both hilt and muzzle boys. Roscommon and Sligo then furnished some of the finest young fellows (fire-eaters) I ever saw; their spirit and decorum were equally admirable, and their honor and liberality conspicuous on all occasions."

In the days of Whitley, the player, there were thirteen families in Connaught, who resented every supposed affront with the death of the offender.

Mr. Moore, in his Memoirs of the Celebrated Irish Chieftain, says "that during what he calls the golden age of jobbing in Ireland, many gentlemen would have considered it a case of 'calling out to be asked what services they performed for their pay.'"

Miss Edgeworth, to whom society is so very much indebted both for amusement and instruction, says the County of Galway was always famous for such fighting gentlemen as, Blue Blaze, Devil Bob, Nineteen-duel Dick, Hair-trigger Pat, and Featherspring Ned.

When Mr. Dillon was shot dead by his adversary, Mr. Kyan, in the forehead, his brother, who was only aged sixteen, very calmly observed that it was a miracle the eye of the deceased was not knocked out. We suppose the gentleman was one of those whose early education had been carefully attended to, as Mr. Kyan, who was a fire-eater, and a celebrated shot himself, lived upon the most intimate terms with the family of Dillon, and had often acted as a second to that gentleman.

While Messrs. Burke and Bodkin, with their seconds, formed a quartette near Glinsk, an old servant thought the group might be improved by carrying the present Sir John Burke, who was then "a child in arms," to see his papa fighting.

Sir Jonah says, "One of the most humane men existing, and a particular friend of mine, and at present a prominent public character, but who (as the expression then was) had frequently played both hilt to hilt, and muzzle to muzzle, was heard endeavouring to keep a little son of his quiet who was crying for something. 'Come now do be a good boy! come now,' said my friend, 'don't cry and we'll *shoot them all* in the morning.' 'Yes, yes, we'll shoot them all in the morning,' responded the child, drying his little eyes, and delighted at the notion.

"Within my recollection, this national propensity for fighting and slaughtering was nearly universal, originating in the spirit and habits of former times. When men had a glowing ambition to excel in all manner of feats and exercises, they naturally conceived, that manslaughter in an *honest* way, (that is not knowing which would be slaughtered) was the most chivalrous and gentlemanly of all their accomplishments; and this idea gave rise to our assiduous cultivation of the arts of combat.

"About the year 1777, the *Fire-eaters'* were in great repute in Ireland—no young fellow could finish his education till he had exchanged shots with some of his acquaintances. The first two questions always asked as to a young man's respectability and qualifications, particularly when he proposed for a lady wife, were—What family is he of? Did he ever blaze?

"Tipperary and Galway were the ablest schools of the duelling science. Galway most scientific at the sword. Tipperary most practical and prized at pistols: Mayo not amiss at either; Roscommon and Sligo had many professors, and a high reputation in the leaden branch of the pastime.

"When I was at the University, Jemmy Keough, Buck English, Cosey Harrison, Crowe Ryan, Reddy Long, Amby Bodkin, Squire Talton, Squire Blake, Amby Fitzgerald, and a few others, were supposed to understand the points of honor better than any men in Ireland, and were constantly referred to.

"In the North, the Fallows and the Fentons were the first hands at it, and most counties could have then boasted their regular point of honor men. The present Chief Justice of the Common Pleas (Norbury) was supposed to have understood the thing as well as any gentleman in Ireland. Every family then had a case of hereditary pistols, which descended as an heir-loom, together with a long silver hilted sword, for the use of their posterity.

"It is incredible what a singular passion the Irish gentlemen (though in general excellent tempered fellows) had formerly for fighting each other, and immediately making friends again. A duel was indeed a necessary piece of a young man's education, but by no means a ground for future animosity with his opponent.

"Men who were libelled generally took the law into their own hands, and eased the King's Bench of great trouble, by the substitution of a small sword for a declaration, or a case of pistols for a judgment.

"Any wanton injury to a tenant was considered as an insult to the lord, and if either of the landlord's sons were grown up, no time was lost by him in demanding satisfaction from any gentleman for the maltreating of even his father's blacksmith. The public used to observe, that a judgment came on Counsellor O'Callaghan, for having kept Mr. Curran quiet in the case of Lord Clanmorris, in as much as his own brains were literally scattered about the ground by an attorney very soon after he had turned pacificator."

An English gentleman, at a Dublin Tavern, having heard some noise proceeding from a wooden partition which stood between his own room and an adjoining one, asked the waiter what occasioned it, and got the following satisfactory explanation, "Oh your honor, it is only my Lord C—— who is pushing with his sword a little, because he expects to fight with some of his best friends who are to be his guests at dinner."

That the evil spirit has not yet been laid in Ireland we could easily demonstrate by a thousand anecdotes and cases which are in our own possession, and which would fully justify our patriotic zeal in bringing several volumes under the notice of reflecting men.

NOTES AND CASES

APOLOGIES

It is a principle which can never be disputed, that he who does an injury should make full reparation, and as Mr. Roscoe has asserted, in his life of Lorenzo de Medicis, no end can justify a sacrifice of principle. No man could refuse ample, and timely reparation, if he had the smallest pretensions to that character which the great English dramatist has sketched.

> "He is complete in manners, and in mind,
> With all good grace, to grace a gentleman."

The Chinese have a proverb "that a fault acknowledged, is half amended," and a celebrated author has declared, that it is almost more honorable to confess a fault, than never to commit one.

Mr. Maurice O'Connel showed more good sense, and feeling, by accepting an apology from Mr. Baker on the ground, than if he slew his adversary under the old Tipperary Code. He may rest assured, that it is not necessary he should fight a duel to establish his character for bravery. He appears not to think that

> "——— Many dangers do environ,
> The man who meddles with cold iron."

Messrs. A. Martin, of Dangan, and T. Blake, of Menlo, were reconciled upon the ground without a shot, by the judicious conduct of their seconds, and very cordially shook hands.

In the case of the American and English officers, at Gibraltar, in July, 1819. Captain Girdlestone, who was second to Captain Johnston, of the 64th regiment, humanely recommended an apology upon the ground, and the parties immediately shook hands.

In the case of Read and Steele, the challenged party would not apologize in Carrickmacross, but on the way to the Isle of Man to fight, an apology was given and received at Newry. The author has this fact from Consellor Kernan, who was one of the seconds.

Major Hillas wrote in very unguarded terms respecting the conduct of Messrs. John and Thomas Fenton, yet he declared even upon the ground, that he would not apologize while his heart beat in his body, and was killed by the first shot of his opponent, John Fenton.

When Sir Alexander Boswell was pressed by his friends to offer an apology, he unfortunately said that an apology was out of the question, and that after what he had written, he had no alternative but fighting. We have many cases in which apologies have been withheld unjustly, and with some of them we might associate the following anecdote.

A man disputing with another, said in a great passion, that he did not like to be thought a scoundrel. I wish, replied his opponent, that you had as great a dislike to the behaviour of a scoundrel.

FATE OF SURVIVORS

What horror, says Hanway, must invade the soul of the surviving duellist; the reproaches of his heart, and his apprehensions of the law, must fill him with dismay: if it was only to die, death is but a debt we owe to nature, and the end of life is to pay that debt in a graceful manner: but under those circumstances it is shocking. Not the devouring flames; nor storms that plunge the affrighted mariner into his watery grave, have half the terrors of this dreadful scene.

Colonel Purefoy having shot a gentleman in a duel at Cork, lost his peace of mind, and became a monument of the folly which prompts mankind to shed a brother's blood in private quarrel.

Previous to Mr. Colclough's fatal duel with Mr. Alcock, a powerful friendship had for many years subsisted between the parties; the tenderest affection had linked the hearts of Colclough and Miss Alcock, who fondly looked to the expected union of their destinies through long and happy times. Colclough was the prop of many an aged widow, and the guardian of every being in his neighbourhood who knew distress. The surrounding heights were covered with anxious spectators of the combat, who offered their prayers in vain for the safety of their long tried friend. Colclough was slain; Miss Alcock's heart was broken; the survivor lost his senses; and in a very short time afterwards was called to that account which every duellist must settle.

Major Campble repeatedly declared himself more miserable than his dying adversary; and although Cecil owed his promotion to the death of Stackpole, whom he shot, he pined and died in four months after the duel.

General Gillespie was never happy after shooting Mr. Barrington. In a letter which we have received from Mr. Brodigan, upon the subject of some fatal duels in America, he describes Mr. Burr, who shot General Hamilton, as care-worn and emaciated; and we could adduce some other cases which would justify the reader in exclaiming:—

"Happy in my mind was he that died,
For many deaths has the survivor suffered."

DISOBEDIENT PRINCIPALS

A second should always quit the field if disobeyed by his principal. In the duel between Capts. D. and S. on Hounslow-heath, the seconds refused to stay upon the ground, because their principals would not be reconciled.

Dr. Dry and Mr. Kearns, acting as the seconds to Frederick E. Jones, Esq. and Capt. Pardy, refused to continue on the ground if the former persisted after the first shot.

We have heard of a case in which Wm. Henry Carroll, Esq. of Dublin, acted with becoming firmness upon the ground.—Mr.

Carroll is a professional gentleman, who has in his own person maintained the point of honor, although he entertains a great abhorrence of duelling, and we believe that he has always used his best exertions to make peace between contending parties, when called upon to act as second.

CHALLENGES WITHDRAWN

Many cases have occurred in which a message has been withdrawn, upon an understanding that such withdrawal would promote an honorable reconciliation. Formerly when a message was withdrawn, the business was supposed to have entirely terminated, and the challenger was erroneously deprived of all redress.

In a case in which we acted as a second to an officer, a message was withdrawn, mutual apologies were offered, and the parties reconciled. A message however must be always cautiously withdrawn.

In the case of Maguire and Leahy, Mr. Crawford, as the second of the former, consented to withdraw the message, upon an understanding that the latter would apologize when such withdrawal had taken place.

REFUSING TO FIRE AT AN INJURED CHALLENGER

Several individuals have received the fire of the challenger without attempting to return it. The Duke of York, who was a warm admirer of our Code, declared he came to the ground for the purpose of satisfying Colonel Lennox, and fired his pistol in the air. The Marquis of Anglesea, whose thanks we also have received for our labours on this subject, refused to fire at Colonel Cadogan, and Captain Garth followed his example, by refusing to fire at Sir Jacob Astley.

"Nothing, surely," says a gallant author, "can be more contemptible, nothing more loudly calls upon the police of every wise government to fix the severest brand of infamy upon it, than the pretended honor of the scoundrel, who, having committed an action confessedly base and unworthy of a gentleman, seeks to silence the universal reproach he has incurred, by murdering the first man that shall express the judgment which all men form of his conduct."

ALTERNATE FIRING

An officer who has written on this subject says, "I will appeal to any one who ever used his pistol, if he can fancy any thing more horrible, or if this vile trick of seconds, in tossing up for the shot, can be taken for any thing less than gambling for the lives of their principals."

A SNAP IS AS GOOD AS A SHOT

In the fatal case of Newburgh and Corry, the former having missed fire, was preparing to make a second effort, when he was informed by his second that a snap was as good as a shot. Several cases of a similar description will be found in the cases we have recorded.

DRAWING BLOOD OR FIRING IN THE AIR

He must have a truly murderous spirit who will fire at any gentleman after he discharges his pistol in the air, and whether swords or pistols are selected, the appearance of blood should generally terminate a duel. A challenged person once demanded another pistol, after the challenger had declared that he was fully satisfied; but the seconds very properly observed, that he "came to give satisfaction, not to take it."

DISUSE OF THE HORSEWHIP

Horse-whipping and posting were amongst the customs which prevailed in Ireland from the good old times, until the publication of this code, but the public taste has undergone a change which need not cause the smallest lamentation.

Amongst the many cases which have been collected for publication, there is one, in which a regimental surgeon, having rashly used a whip, was willing to place it in the hand of the challenger, with a suitable apology, but dreaded his doing such an act of justice might deprive himself and family of their subsistence, when the circumstance should come to the knowledge of his brother officers. His generous adversary said, "let me have it under his own hand that the performance of his duty, will be injurious to my family, and certainly the whip shall be dispensed with."

The author has been assured by the second to Counsellor Hatchell, in a duel which unfortunately proved fatal to Mr. Morley, that with the Counsellor's humane permission, he offered to take an apology, and wave his right to return the slight assault which his adversary had committed on his cheek with a glove. The circumstance is highly honorable to Mr. Hatchell, who found himself committed with a very positive antagonist, and the father of a very numerous family.

In the fatal case of Blake and Burke, although a horse-whip had been used by Burke, the former would have taken any reasonable apology, but the latter fell a victim to his obstinacy.

DECIDING ELECTIONS BY A SHOT

Had John Colclough acted with a due regard to the interests which he professed to support, he would have said to the second of his adversary, "Sir, I have had no personal difference with my good friend Alcock, we have always lived on terms of the kindest intimacy, and I see no reason for deciding our contest for the representation of the County of Wexford by a duel. Independent of the deep regret which I should feel through life, in the event of his being killed by me, I owe it to the freeholders, who are zealous for my return, not to hazard their defeat by such a rash decision.

DANGER OF PUBLICITY

In the case of O'Connell, sen. and D' Esterre, it is impossible to calculate on the result had Mr. O'Connell fallen. The duel was forced upon him wantonly by his opponent, every publicity was given to the breach, and the fatal field was surrounded by many thousand of those "children of impulse," who considered the learned gentleman as the champion of their creed and country. Who then could have restrained them? We are decidedly of opinion, that the duel should not have taken place. O'Connell had no personal difference with D' Esterre, and had he been so rash as to assault the Counsellor, the latter should have brought him before the Court of King's Bench, as the fearless Curran did upon a similar occasion. Circumstances however, which shall be explained hereafter, influenced Mr. O'Connell to show he did not wear a "snow white feather in his helmet," and he killed D' Esterre.

DIMINISHING THE MARK

Amongst the errors committed in the case of Bric, was that of giving the word to fire by Mr. Bric's own second, while his principal was in the act of apologising for an awkwardness, arising from his inexperience in the field, his front was exposed to the fire of his opponent, who without any extraordinary haste, might have shot him before he could have raised his pistol. He was a victim of mismanagement from the beginning.

Messrs. O'Ferrall and Fenton, who acted as seconds in the case of Major Hillas and Mr. John Fenton, squared the principals, in order to present the smallest possible objects. Major Hillas threw off his coat upon the ground, and appeared with light black sleeves attached to his waistcoat, evidently with a view to present the less conspicuous object to his adversary. The reason Major Hillas had black sleeves attached to his waistcoat, was to make his bulk appear the smaller. There is another mode of lessening the object to be fired at, which is thus described by a military officer who has written on the present subject, "By advancing the foot, and inclining in the act of presenting, the body will be lowered some inches, and many is the good or bad head that had been saved by it."

DISTANCE

In the case of Major Hillas and Mr. Fenton, spud stones were placed to mark the distance, and prevent the parties from advancing toward each other.

An officer, who has written on the subject, says "the distance being a matter entirely in the breasts of the seconds, where neither heat nor animosity can be supposed to exist, one cannot but wonder at the bloody distances which are sometimes given; eight and seven yards are not unfrequent; and which, when the parties come to present, will of course bring the mouths of the pistols to no more than four or five.

"And if this be not bringing their friends to an impossibility of escaping, any man of skill shall determine.

"Strange it is to think how the seconds can ever be induced to act in so desperate a manner, or on what kind of principles they can possibly proceed. Have they really such a cool, diabolical design as to bring certain death to one or the other of their friends? Can they not be satisfied with giving a fair and gentleman-like distance, which may sufficiently atone for any offence, and yet leave some kind of chance for their escaping and living for an honorable reconciliation.

"Charity must lead us to hope that the seconds, who have hitherto committed such mistakes, can only have erred through ignorance or inconsideration; and that when it is properly represented to them, they will be reclaimed from such unreasonable and bloody proceedings. As matters of this kind are wisely taken from the power of the principals; it is earnestly to be hoped, that the seconds will in future shew greater consideration and respect for the lives and eternal welfare of their friends.

"But it often happens, from want of caution in the second, that when ten yards are agreed on, yet still the parties fight at eight; and this is occasioned by their being left without particular orders for the advanced foot in presenting, for if they step beyond, instead of to the mark of distance, they clearly gain a yard upon each other.

"The second ought always to place a good and sufficient mark, and give positive order for no advance beyond it, when they come to fire."

When the present Counsellor Kernan was in the army, and fought Captain Sandys, the latter would have no second. He insisted upon fighting at six yards, and charged his pistol for that distance, at which he was almost certain he should hit the fourteenth man. But the Surgeon-General who attended to see that all was fair, joined Mr. Kernan's second in protesting against less than a dozen paces, which saved the life of Kernan at the first discharge, as he was very slightly wounded in the side by a ball, which would easily have pierced his heart at six yards distance.

After Mr. Kernan came to the bar, he was second to a Mr. Fitzgerald an attorney, and the opposing second having choice of ground insisted upon seven paces, K. replied that as the combatants were tall he would object to such a short distance, and leave the ground.

Mr. K. was also a friend to Mr. Robert Hickson, when challenged by a Mr. Prendergast, and having the appointment of the
distance, he named twelve paces. The friend of Mr. P. insisted
on their walking towards each other, and firing at discretion, and
Mr. K. unable to dissuade the adverse party from so bloody a
proceeding marched his friend away with the cordial approbation of the disinterested persons present.

Surely when such men as Lord Camelford, and Captain Best,
fought their fatal duel, at full thirty paces, and when the pistols
will kill at a much greater distance, it is a wanton sporting with
existence to fight at ten or twelve yards distance.

SLIGHTED CHALLENGES

A few years since, a Baronet in England refused to meet a
gentleman

> "whose rank
> Was slight, unless nobility of soul,
> Might cope with blazoned scutcheons."

The friends of the slighted gentleman published their opinion
of his character—the public feeling became so strong against
the Baronet, that he changed his mind, and avowed his willingness to fight; but he found it was too late, for the friends of the
slighted gentleman, very properly refused to let him meet the
Baronet, and thus the imputed stain was very happily trans-
ferred. The Baronet does not now enjoy the character of
Bayard, *"Le Chevalier sans peur et sans reproche."* Though his
adversary retain,

> "no sign,
> Save men's opinions, and his living blood,
> To shew the world he is a gentleman."

Lieutenant Johnston, was not quite so fortunate at Youghal,
where though he had most wantonly insulted Mr. Thomas Barry,
he refused to meet him or apologize, because he was the son of
an apothecary. It was referred however to the Earl of Shannon,
who declared that he would if challenged by Mr. Barry, jun.

have no objection to attend the call, the parties met and Johnston was the victim of his rashness, and injustice.

Mr. Heaviside, the surgeon, was committed to Newgate on a charge of murder, by Mr. Forde, the Magistrate, although he only had attended in his professional capacity. Bail to a heavy amount was offered for the surgeon, but refused by Mr. Forde, who declared that in future he would commit all persons who were present at a fatal duel. When a surgeon or bystander is under such a great responsibility, who can question his right to offer a conciliatory opinion, even though unasked.

If the responsibility of bystanders be great, so is the power with which the law invests them. Blackstone says, "an affray, or fight, between two or more persons in a public place, may be suppressed by any person present, who is justifiable in endeavouring to part the combatants, whatever consequences may ensue. The punishment for common affrays, is by fine and imprisonment; the measure of which must be regulated by the circumstances of the case: for, where there is any material aggravation, the punishment proportionally increases. As where two persons coolly and deliberately engage in a duel: this, being attended with an apparent intention, and danger of murder, and being a high contempt of the justice of the nation, is a strong aggravation of the affray, though no mischief has actually ensued."

JOKES AND HORSE PLAY

It has been very justly said that too much familiarity breeds contempt; and gentlemen should very carefully preserve that decency of language and behaviour which is perfectly consistent with the strongest friendship.

In No. 429 of the Spectator, there is an excellent article upon the impropriety of too great familiarity between acquaintances, which we would recommend for general consideration.

Harvey Aston had many good qualities, but he had a most inordinate disposition to quizzing, which involved him in many personal encounters, whereby he obtained the reputation of a professed duellist, several years before he fell a victim to the practice.

Amongst the interesting cases which we have collected, there is a melancholy one which occurred between Messrs. French and Dillon, two young gentlemen, who, with others, were amusing themselves at leapfrog, on the lawn of Mr. Plunket's hospitable Irish mansion, near Roscommon.

Major Glover of the Lincolnshire Militia, was at the rehearsal of a play at Manchester, in May, 1760. Mr. Jackson, an apothecary, came behind, and struck the Major, apparently in a joke; the major turned round, and with a switch struck Mr. Jackson, saying also as a joke, "What, Jackson, is it you?" upon which Jackson in a great passion said, "D—n you Sir, though you are a Major, I will not take this from you." The Major surprised, replied, "Why, what can you mean? I was only in joke as well as yourself." Jackson insisted on a meeting afterwards, and could not be pacified. They went to a private room at a coffee-house, where Jackson was mortally wounded through the body; after which Major Glover led him through the coffee-room, looking for assistance, and Mr. Jackson acknowledged that he only was to blame.

In the case of Keefe and Fitzgerald, at Athy, the former had been horsewhipped by the latter, and a reconciliation had taken place; but Fitzgerald unfortunately shot some nuts across a table at Mr. Keefe in playfulness, which revived the recollection of the former quarrel; and led to the death of Mr. Fitzgerald at the first shot. Another instance of the fatal effects of horse play.

SEASON AND WEATHER

A gentleman should not be so situated on the ground, as to have the wind, dust, sleet, snow, rain, hail, or sun in his face.

ONE SECOND

When Messrs. John Kemble and Aikin fought, the elder Mr. Bannister was second to them both, which was rather a hazardous undertaking.

PISTOLS

Should invariably be preferred to swords. "I have often blessed Beau Nash," says O'Keefe in his Recollections, "for abolishing swords. Challenges and pistol work are bad enough; but even then the wrathful man may have a chance of a watchful Providence not permitting the sun to go down upon his anger."

Rifles should always be rejected, or pistol barrels mounted upon carbine stocks. The charging should be conducted by one of the seconds in the presence of the other, or as both are chosen for their high sense of honor and good feeling for the parties, each second may be allowed to charge the pistol for the opposing principal. The seconds of Lords Wellington and Winchelsea, gave the charging of the pistols to the surgeon in attendance. No pistol should contain two bullets, or such as being rough externally may make a wound unnecessarily dangerous. The wadding should not be such as might accompany the ball, as the smallest portion of extraneous matter, if unextracted by the surgeon, may lead to gangrene and to death. The pistols should not be cocked, nor have their feather springs set when given to the combatants, nor should two pistols be delivered at a time.

DOUBLE DUELS

No gentleman should be allowed to fight two different adversaries for the same offence. When Mr. Long Wellesley fought Mr. Crespigny, at Calais, for an offence which had been given to his father, the brother endeavoured to obtain a similar satisfaction, to which Mr. Wellesley had consented; but the seconds, Colonel Freemantle and Captain Brooke, of the Guards, declared that Mr. W. having done all which could be reasonably expected, he should not fight the brother of his adversary, and all left the ground.

WRITTEN STATEMENTS

The whole cause of quarrel should be found accurately stated in the challenge and reply, and the description of the duel should be under the signatures of both the seconds. In cases, however, where the seconds cannot agree exactly, after a reference to by-standers, either of them may temperately commit himself on the disputed point by stating his individual impressions, at which the other cannot reasonably take offence, as two eye-witnesses of the same transaction may conscientiously dissent in its description.

GENEROSITY OF COMBATANTS

Mr. Clive, afterwards Lord Clive, having a quarrel about a gambling debt in India, his opponent reserved his fire, walked up to him and said, "Ask your life, retract, and pay the money."—"Fire and be d—d," said Clive, upon which his adversary said he was too brave a fellow to be shot.

When Messrs. Macloghlin and O'Meara were both desperately and similarly wounded, the former having first anxiously enquired respecting the fate of his opponent, expressed his hope that he was not in such agony as he himself endured.

When a member of the American Congress shot Doctor Carson, the latter expressed great satisfaction on being informed that his opponent had escaped uninjured.

Harvey Aston when mortally wounded in the spine by Colonel Allen, took deliberate aim at his opponent, and then lowering his pistol said, I could kill him, but the last act of my life shall not be an act of revenge.

Mutual forgiveness, and a cordial reconciliation of the parties, must always be highly influential in the recovery from wounds.

COURAGE

Having much to say upon this subject in the second volume, we shall content ourselves at present by quoting two or three authorities, which are worthy of consideration.

"Courage," says a public writer, "is a firm, and constant disposition of mind, whereby a man is fixed, and determined, never to dread any evil so far as to decline it, when the choosing it is the only remedy against a greater."

Shakspeare says,

"Rightly to be great,
Is not to stir without great argument."

It has been very justly said by another of our poets,

"Who wickedly is wise, or madly brave,
Is but the more a fool, the more a knave."

BOASTERS

A gentleman was killed a few years since in Ireland, after slitting his cane with a pistol ball, and inviting his friends to go and see him shoot *a crow of an attorney*.

An English and a French officer quarrelled at Bourdeaux, in 1824. The Englishman wagered a dozen of Champaigne, that at the first shot he would shave the mustachio of his adversary.

Hold your jaw said a boaster once in the lobby of Drury Lane theatre, or I will put you between two pieces of bread and butter, and eat you up like an anchovy.

We could give several instances of bad taste like the preceding ones, and other cases in which a single shade of gentlemanly conduct could not possibly be traced. In the succeeding volumes they will be found under some of the following heads—Honor, Courage, Cowardice, Gentlemen, Murderers, Ruffians, Female Duels, Ludicrous Duels, Naval Duels, Military Duels, Electioneering Duels, Parliamentary Duels, Political Duels, National Duels, Lawyers' Duels, Clergymens' Duels, Tavern Duels, or in the Appendix, for which suggestions are requested.

COURT OF CHIVALRY

Judge Blackstone says, "it requires such a degree of passive valour, to combat the dread of even undeserved contempt, arising from the false notions of honor too generally received in Europe, that the strongest prohibitions and penalties of the law will never be entirely effectual to eradicate this unhappy custom, till a method be found of compelling the original aggressor to make some other satisfaction to the affronted party, which the world shall esteem equally reputable as that which is now given at the hazard of the life and fortune, as well of the person insulted as of him who hath given the insult."

"The Court of Chivalry in England has fallen into entire disuse, there having been no permanent High Constable since the execution of Stafford, Duke of Buckingham, in the reign of Henry VIII. The authority and charge of this court was so ample for a subject, that when Chief Justice Fineux was asked by Henry how far they extended, he declined answering; and said, the decision of that question belonged to the law of arms, and not to the law of England.

"The court was formerly held before the Lord High Constable and Earl Marshal of England jointly, but since the attainder of Stafford, and the consequent extinguishment of the office of Lord High Constable, it hath usually, with respect to civil matters, been held before the Earl Marshal only. This court, by statute 13, Ric. ii. c. 2, hath cognizance of contracts and other matters touching deeds of arms and war, as well out of the realm as within it, and from its sentence an appeal was immediately to the king in person. The court was in great reputation in the times of pure chivalry, and afterwards during our connection with the continent, by the territories which our princes held in France: but is now grown almost entirely out of use, on account of the feebleness of its jurisdiction, and want of power to enforce its judgments; as it can neither fine nor imprison, not being a court of record."

Its jurisdiction as a Court of Honor, lay in giving satisfaction to all those who were aggrieved in points which were so delicate in their nature as to include wrongs and injuries which escape the notice of the common law, and yet require some species of redress, such as using the term coward to a soldier, or liar to a gentleman, for which no action will lie in the courts at Westminster or Dublin; but this court could never interfere in any matter which was determinable by the common law. It could only compel the defendant "Mendicium sibi ipsi imponere," or to take upon himself the lie which he had given, or make such other submission as the laws of honor might require.

ANTI-DUELLISTS

Many individuals of rank or talent have expressed themselves upon the practice of duelling.

Hervey says, "What mortal feuds, what cruel bloodshed, what terrible slaughterdom have been committed for the point of honor, and some courtly ceremonies."

Another author says, "If men fought only when they could not be at peace, there would be very little fighting in the world."

"If" says the Prince of Conte, "those who fight duels, were never spoken of but as fools and mad-men, as indeed they are, if that phantom of honor, which is their idol, was never represented but as a chimera and a folly, if care was taken never to form any image of revenge, but as a mean and cowardly action; the resentment which men feel upon an affront, would be infinitely weaker; but that which exasperates and renders it the more lively, is the false impression that there is cowardice in braving an affront."

"There is no man (says Hanway,) who acts virtuously, but some body or other suffers when he dies: however let us consider him in the different relations of life; suppose him wedded to a woman of honor and sentiment, a kind husband, a dutiful son, a tender parent, faithful friend, and except in his wild enthusiasm a sincere lover of his country. Behold him prostrate on the earth, killed by the hand of him who perhaps was yesterday the friend of his bosom, and a man whom he wished to serve; sent to his last account with all his sins upon him; plunged into eternity in a rebellious act against the plain decrees of Heaven. Whilst we see the blood issuing from his wound, behold the gentle matron, the partner of all his happiness or misery, with floods of tears streaming from her eyes, calling for that aid which now no mortal hand can give her; the tender infant by her side, knows not that one fatal thrust robs him of all the joys, the comforts and support with which providence had blessed him in a parent now no more. The aged father losing a son in whom all his worldly joys were centered, and for whom only he desired to live, droops his heavy head, and dies with sorrow."

"It is no uncommon thing with persons of duelling propensity, to make a very liberal but inexplicable use of the term satisfaction. An honest country gentleman had the misfortune to fall into company with two or three modern men of honor, where he happened to be very ill treated. One of the company, being conscious of the offence, sent him a note the following morning, and informed him that he was ready to give him satisfaction. 'Why surely now' said the plain honest man, 'this is a fine affair, last night he sent me away very much offended and out of temper, and this morning he fancies it would be a satisfaction to me that he should run his sword through my body.'"

Harvey Aston used to say, "I was in the theatre one night, and seeing a fellow eating apples in the box where there were some ladies, I took the liberty of poking one into his throat with my finger: the man struck me, I knocked him down and gave him a sound drubbing (for the Colonel was a famous bruiser and a patron of the fancy,) he called me out, I shot him through the arm, and the fool called that satisfaction."

Major Hillas, on coming to the ground, near Sligo, said "I am sorry the mistaken laws of honor oblige me to come here to defend myself, and I declare I have no animosity to any man or woman on the face of the earth."

During the administration of Lord Talbot in Ireland, an officer of the name of Verner, or Vernon, received a challenge from a gentleman, who was generally admitted to be as fond of quarrelling as he was remarkable for the accuracy of his aim, and having submitted to the good sense of his brother officers, he declined the invitation to the field. His excellency to mark his approbation of this forbearance, immediately appointed Mr. V. one of his aid-de-camps.

Although we have some cases ready for the press in which we have been personally interested, we have purposely abstained from noticing them at present, and trust that the justice, generosity, or patriotism of the gentlemen whose names are of necessity associated with those cases, may supersede the necessity for our doing justice to ourselves. We express this hope in the temperate and amicable spirit which dictated the Dedication of our Reflections upon Duelling, as it has been copied into page v of the Introduction, particularly as the parties now alluded to, are heads of interesting families, and not much stronger advocates for single combat than ourselves.